NAPOLEON HILL'S
SPEAK IT
INTO
REALITY

T0398100

sound
wisdom.
Because Your Success Matters

NAPOLEON HILL'S

SPEAK IT
INTO
REALITY

ACHIEVE YOUR
GOALS THROUGH THE
POWER OF FAITH
AND WORDS

AN OFFICIAL PUBLICATION OF THE

NAPOLEON HILL FOUNDATION®

Published and distributed by:

SOUND WISDOM
P.O. Box 310
Shippensburg, PA 17257-0310

717-530-2122

info@soundwisdom.com

www.soundwisdom.com

ISBN 13 TP: 978-1-64095-632-2

ISBN 13 eBook: 978-1-64095-633-9

For Worldwide Distribution, Printed in the U.S.A.

1 2 3 4 5 6 7 8 / 29 28 27 26 25

CONTENTS

INTRODUCTION

Napoleon Hill is the author of *Think and Grow Rich* (over 100 million copies sold!), *Master Key to Riches,* and other best-selling books. He is also the creator of the American Philosophy of Individual Achievement. His discussion on "going the extra mile" has made hundreds of thousands of wealthy men and women worldwide who have taken the time to put his wisdom into practice in their lives.

Every person needs a philosophy of life, and in Dr. Hill's books you will find the principles to guide you and sustain you in whatever work you have chosen. His philosophy does not conflict in any way with your religion or your political beliefs–but rather augments and amplifies them.

Although written a few decades ago, the wisdom, advice, humor, and proven-successful strategies are just as relevant now than they were then–in fact, even more so.

Speak It Into Reality shares the power of "autosuggestion" and other successful approaches to living your best life. This mini but mighty book is a guide inspired by Napoleon Hill's timeless principles. Learn how the words you speak and the thoughts you hold can reprogram your subconscious, empowering you to achieve your greatest goals.

This book dives into the science and philosophy behind autosuggestion, reveals how faith, belief, and repetition can shape your reality, and the delves into the importance of your words. You will learn how to:

- Craft affirmations that rewire your subconscious for success.

- Develop unwavering faith in your goals and dreams.

- Leverage the emotions of love and confidence to amplify your affirmations.

- Overcome negative thought patterns and replace them with positive intentions.

Whether you're striving for financial success, personal growth, or spiritual fulfillment, this book provides the tools to transform your mindset and speak your dreams into existence. Start changing your reality—one word at a time.

We at the Napoleon Hill Foundation hope this mini-book will inspire you to look into Napoleon Hill's original books that delve more deeply into matters of personal achievement, helping you reach that point in life when all of your plans have been fulfilled and you achieve every goal.

Don M. Green
Chief Executive Officer and Executive Director
Napoleon Hill Foundation

1

IGNITE YOUR BURNING DESIRE

A long while ago, a great warrior faced a situation that made it necessary for him to make a decision that ensured his success on the battlefield. He was about to send his armies against a powerful foe, whose men outnumbered his own. He loaded his soldiers into boats, sailed to the enemy's country, unloaded soldiers and equipment, then gave the order to burn the ships that had carried them.

Addressing his men before the first battle, he said, "You see the boats going up in smoke. That means we cannot leave these shores alive unless we win! We now have no choice—we win—or we perish!" They won.

Every person who wins in any undertaking must be willing to burn their ships and cut all sources of retreat. Only by so doing can we be sure of maintaining the state of mind known as a *burning desire to win*, which is essential to success.

The following are 11 principles,[1] the basis of how to think and grow rich by speaking into reality your desired ambitions and future. These fundamental standards are the foundation on which all wealth and riches are built:

1. **Desire.** A burning desire to achieve your goals fuels your motivation and commitment. Defining your objectives and envisioning their realization is your jumping off point into your vision of the future.

2. **Faith.** A passionate belief in your ability to succeed empowers you to overcome obstacles and maintain motivation.

3. **Autosuggestion.** Positive affirmations and self-talk reinforces your beliefs and form your reality. Visualizing your goals as if they are already achieved is paramount for success.

4. **Specialized Knowledge.** Relevant knowledge and skills help you reach your goals, as will life-long learning and remaining flexible.

5. **Imagination.** Opening yourself to being creative and using your imagination will take you to

---

1. In Napoleon Hill's worldwide well-known book, *Think and Grow Rich,* he explains his 13 principles in great detail, summarized here.

yet-unknown levels of success. Learning to think creatively is crucial, and fun!

6. **Organized Planning.** Setting goals and objectives and writing detailed, well-planned steps will carry to from one achievement to the next to the next....

7. **Decisionmaking.** Wise, prompt, decisive actions are vital when speaking your goals into reality.

8. **Persistence.** Determined, persistent commitment is required to solve problems and face challenges while advancing toward your goals.

9. **Mastermind Alliance.** A mastermind alliance is a combination of intelligent and creative people who share and support each other with ideas and wisdom to achieve a common goal.

10. **Subconsciousness.** Learning how to use the power of your subconscious mind is the key to speaking your desires into reality. Your inner self, your intuition, adds a dimension to your life that you can use for great benefit.

11. **Conquering Fear.** Many people are paralyzed with fear. Overcoming fear unlocks the doors holding you back from stepping into your God-given future of health and wealth.

Wishing does not bring riches.

Every human being who reaches the age of understanding of the purpose of money, wishes for it. Wishing will not bring riches. But desiring riches with a state of mind that becomes an obsession, then planning definite ways and means to acquire riches, and backing those plans with persistence that does not recognize failure will bring riches.

Those who become "money conscious" accumulate great riches. "Money consciousness" means that the mind has become so thoroughly saturated with the *desire* for money that people can see themselves as already in possession of it.

The steps to this mindset call for no "hard labor" and no sacrifice. The steps do not require you to become ridiculous or credulous. To apply the steps calls for no great amount of education. But the successful application of the following six steps does demand sufficient imagination to enable you to see and understand that the accumulation of money cannot be left to chance, good fortune, or luck. You must realize that all who have accumulated great fortunes first did a certain amount of *dreaming, hoping, wishing, desiring, and planning* before they acquired money.

The method by which *desire* for riches can be transmuted into its material equivalent consists of six definite, practical steps. Note that the formula applies equally to any form of wealth, whether relational, professional, intellectual, financial, or otherwise.

First. Fix in your mind the exact amount of money you desire. It is not sufficient merely to say "I want plenty of money." Be definite as to the amount. (There is a psychological reason for definiteness that is described in a subsequent chapter.)

Second. Determine exactly what you intend to give in return for the money you desire. (There is no such reality as something for nothing.)

Third. Establish a definite date by which you intend to possess the money you desire.

Fourth. Create a definite plan for carrying out your desire, and begin at once, whether you are ready or not, to put this plan into action.

Fifth. Write out a clear, concise statement of the amount of money you intend to acquire, name the time limit for its acquisition, state what you intend to give in return for the money, and describe clearly the plan through which you intend to accumulate it.

Sixth. Read your written statement aloud twice daily, once just before retiring at night and once after waking up in the morning. *As you read, see, feel, and believe yourself to be already in possession of the money.* Speak it into reality!

It is important that you follow the instructions described in these six steps. It is especially important that you observe and follow the instructions in the sixth paragraph. You may complain that it is impossible for you to "see yourself in possession of money" before you actually have it, but here is where a *burning desire* will come to your aid.

If you truly *desire* money so keenly that your desire is an obsession, then you will have no difficulty in convincing yourself that you will acquire it. The object is to want money (or whatever your primary definite aim is) and to become so determined to have it that you *convince* yourself you will have it.

If you do not see great riches in your imagination, you will never see them in your bank balance.

Tolerance and an open mind are practical necessities for today's dreamer. Those who are afraid of new ideas are doomed before they start. Never has there been a time more favorable to pioneers than the present. True, there is no wild and woolly West to be conquered, but there are vast business, financial, industrial, and cyberspace worlds to be explored, remolded, and redirected along new and better lines.

Awake, arise, and assert yourself, you world dreamer. Your star is now ascending. The world's economic crises create opportunities for innovation and greatness. They teach people humility, tolerance, and open-mindedness.

> **If you don't see great riches in your imagination, you won't see it in your bank account.**

The world is filled with an abundance of opportunity that the dreamers of the past never knew.

We who are in this race for riches should be encouraged to know that this changed world in which we live is demanding new ideas, new ways of doing things, new leaders, new inventions, new methods of teaching, new methods of marketing, new books, new literature, new features for the radio and television, new ideas for movies and other media.

Behind all this demand for new and better, there are three qualities you must possess to win:

1. Definiteness of purpose

2. Knowledge of what you want

3. A burning *desire* to possess it

The recession in 1929-1939 marked the death of one age and the birth of another. This changed world required practical dreamers who could and did put their dreams into action. The practical dreamers have always been, and always will be, the pattern makers of civilization.

A *burning desire to be and to do* is the starting point from which the dreamer must take off. Dreams are not born of indifference, laziness, or lack of ambition.

How can you harness and use the power of desire? This question has been answered through this and the subsequent chapters of this book. This message is going out to the world during tumultuous times. It is reasonable to presume that the message may come to the attention of many who have been wounded by the economic chaos, those who have lost their fortunes, others who have lost their positions, and great numbers who must reorganize their plans and stage a comeback. To all these people I convey the thought that all achievement, no matter what may be its nature or purpose, must begin with an intense burning desire for something definite.

> **All achievement begins with an intense burning desire for something definite.**

Through some strange and powerful principle of "mental chemistry" never divulged, Nature wraps up in the impulse of strong desire "that certain something" that recognizes no such word as "impossible" and accepts no such reality as "failure."

There is a difference between *wishing* for something and being *ready* to receive it. No one is ready for anything until they believe that they can acquire it. The state of mind must be *belief*, not mere hoping or wishing. Open-mindedness is essential for belief. Closed minds do not inspire faith, courage, and belief.

Remember, no more effort is required to aim high in life, to demand abundance and prosperity, than is required to accept misery and poverty.

Success begins with setting a definite goal.

I encourage you to write a clear, concise statement of your definite major purpose. Be specific. If it's monetary, write the exact amount you wish to acquire. Establish a date by which you plan to attain your definite chief aim. Speak your statement aloud twice per day. As you verbally say the words, see it, feel it, and believe yourself to be already in possession of your desire.

If you do not see great riches in your imagination, you will never see them in your bank balance. Will you begin today to believe it to see it? Never in the history of the world has there been so great an opportunity for practical dreamers as now exists.

The world we live in is demanding new ideas, new inventions, and new ways of doing things. This means opportunity. To capitalize on these ever-emerging opportunities, you must possess definiteness of purpose, the knowledge of what you want, and a burning desire to possess it.

A burning desire to be and to do is the starting point from which you, the dreamer, must take off.

QUESTIONS TO CONSIDER

1. What is my definite goal, my burning desire that needs to be ignited?

_____

_____

_____

_____

2. Everyone who has accumulated great fortunes first did a certain amount of *dreaming, hoping, wishing, desiring, and planning* before they acquired money. How much dreaming, hoping, wishing, desiring, and planning have I done so far? Enough?

_____

_____

_____

_____

_____

3. How willing am I to dream and know that my dreams can actually come true? Am I a "practical dreamer" who can write a concise statement of my purpose in life and my current goals?

_____

_____

_____

_____

_____

4. Because no one is ready to receive until they believe they can have it, do I believe that the desire I want is mine already?

_____

_____

_____

_____

_____

_____

5. Closed minds do not inspire faith, courage, and belief. How open-minded am I?

_____

_____

_____

_____

_____

_____

2

FAITH'S REALITY

There are millions of people who *believe* that they are "doomed" to poverty and failure because of some strange force over which they *believe* they have no control. They are the creators of their own "misfortunes" because of this negative *belief*, which is picked up by the subconscious mind and translated into its physical equivalent.

Throughout the ages, people have instructed their struggling friends to "Have faith," but they have failed to speak reality to them about *how* to have faith. They have not stated or understood that *faith is a state of mind that may be induced by self-suggestion.*

Faith is the visualization and declaration of and belief in the attainment of desire. Faith is a state of mind that may be induced, or created, by affirmation or repeated instructions to the subconscious mind through the principle of autosuggestion (self-suggestion).

As an illustration of faith, consider why you are, presumably, reading this book. The object is, naturally, to acquire the ability to transmute the intangible thought impulse of desire into its physical counterpart, money, success, or whatever your personal goal.

By following the instructions in the next chapters on autosuggestion and the subconscious mind, you can *convince* your subconscious mind that you *believe* you will receive what you are asking for, and it will act upon that belief. Your subconscious mind will pass back to you in the form of "faith," followed by definite plans for procuring what you desire.

> **Speaking affirmation repeatedly directed toward your subconscious mind is the only method of voluntary development of the emotion of faith.**

The method by which you develop *faith,* where it does not already exist, is difficult to describe. Faith is a state of mind that you may develop after you master and apply the principles, or steps, discussed throughout this book. The repetition of affirmations about the certainty of your success–directed toward your subconscious mind–is the only known method of voluntary development of the emotion of faith.

The meaning of faith may be made clearer through the following explanation of the way people sometimes become criminals. Stated in the words of a famous criminologist: "When men first come into contact with crime, they abhor it. If they remain in contact with crime for a time, they become accustomed to it, and endure it. If they remain in contact with it long enough, they finally embrace it, and become influenced by it."

This is the equivalent of saying that any impulse of thought that is repeatedly passed on to the subconscious mind is, finally, accepted and acted upon by the subconscious mind. It then proceeds to translate that impulse into its physical equivalent by the most practical procedure available.

In connection with this, consider the statement: All thoughts that have been emotionalized (given feeling) and mixed with faith begin immediately to translate themselves into their physical equivalent or counterpart.

> **Emotionalized thoughts mixed with faith immediately translate physically.**

The emotions, or the "feeling" portion of thoughts, are the factors that give thoughts vitality, life, and action. The emotions of faith, love, and sex—when mixed with any thought impulse—give it greater action than any of these emotions can do singly.

Not only thought impulses that have been mixed with faith, but those mixed with any positive or negative emotion may reach and influence the subconscious mind. From this statement, you will understand that the subconscious mind translates into its physical equivalent a thought impulse of a negative or destructive nature, just as readily as it acts upon thought impulses of a positive or constructive nature. This accounts for the strange phenomenon referred to as "misfortune" or "bad luck" that so many millions of people experience.

Emotionalized thoughts mixed with faith immediately translate physically.

> # Faith is a state of mind induced by self-suggestion.

Always remember to have faith in yourself and faith in the Infinite. And remember:

- Faith is the "eternal elixir" that gives life, power, and action to the impulse of thought!

- The previous sentence is worth reading a second time, and a third, and a fourth. It is worth reading aloud!

- Faith is the starting point of all accumulation of riches!

- Faith is the basis of all "miracles" and all mysteries that cannot be analyzed by the rules of science!

- Faith is the only known antidote for failure!

- Faith is the element, the "chemical," that when mixed with prayer, gives you direct communication with Infinite Intelligence.

- Faith is the element that transforms the ordinary vibration of thought, created by the finite mind of humans, into its spiritual equivalent.

- Faith is the only agency through which the force of Infinite Intelligence can be harnessed and used by you.

Every one of these statements is provable!

> # Resolve to throw off negative influences and build your positive life.

The following is a Self-Confidence Formula. There are five affirmations that are important to absorb into your mindset and then apply to your everyday life. Find a quiet, private place, and write down each component of the formula; then speak each one aloud–confidently. Speak it into reality.

> **First.** I know that I have the ability to achieve the object of my definite purpose in life; therefore, I *demand* of myself persistent, continuous action toward its attainment, and I here and now promise to render such action. I will state my purpose routinely.

Second. I realize that the dominating thoughts of my mind will eventually reproduce themselves in outward, physical action, and gradually transform themselves into material reality; therefore, I will concentrate my thoughts for 30 minutes daily upon the task of thinking of the person I intend to become, thereby creating in my mind a clear mental picture of that person. I will also describe myself verbally to cement that picture.

Third. I know through the principle of self-suggestion any desire I persistently hold in my mind will eventually seek expression through some practical means of attaining the object behind it; therefore, I will devote ten minutes daily to demanding of myself the development of self-confidence by declaring such.

Fourth. I have clearly written down a description of my definite chief aim in life, and I will never stop trying to achieve it. I will develop sufficient self-confidence for its attainment.

Fifth. I fully realize that no wealth or position can long endure unless built upon truth and justice; therefore, I will engage in no transaction that does not benefit all whom it affects. I will succeed by attracting to myself the forces I wish to use and the cooperation of other people. I will induce others to assist me, because of my willingness to serve others. I will eliminate hatred, envy, jealousy, selfishness, and cynicism by developing and declaring love for all humanity, because I know that a negative attitude and speech toward others can never bring me success. I will cause others to believe in me, because I will believe in them and in myself.

I will sign my name to this formula, commit it to memory, and repeat it aloud once a day with full *faith* that it will gradually influence my *thoughts and actions and words* so I will become a self-reliant and successful person. This formula has at its basis a law of nature, autosuggestion.

Develop the self-confidence necessary to achieve your definite chief aim by activating the law of autosuggestion to convince yourself—and thus your subconscious mind—of the certainty of your eventual success!

QUESTIONS TO CONSIDER

1. Because faith is a state of mind that may be induced, or created, by affirmation or repeated instructions to the subconscious mind, how "faithful" do you consider yourself to be regarding: your relationships; your career; your financial status?

---

2. As all thoughts that are emotionalized and mixed with faith immediately begin to translate into a physical equivalent or counterpart, where are your thoughts taking you? Providing for you?

---

3. Your belief, or faith, determines the action of your subconscious mind. What actions have you taken lately that are direct results of your belief and faith?

_____

_____

_____

_____

_____

_____

4. There are millions of people who believe that they are "doomed" to poverty and failure because of some strange force over which they believe they have no control. They are the creators of their own misfortune. True? Are you one of the millions?

_____

_____

_____

_____

_____

_____

5. Faith is the starting point of all accumulation of riches; likewise, no faith produces no riches. Where to you fall in line with that statement?

_____

_____

_____

_____

_____

_____

6. Because faith gives life, power, and action to the impulse of thought, do you realize that your thoughts are full of life, powerful, and actionable?

_____

_____

_____

_____

_____

_____

7. The subconscious mind translates into reality a thought driven by fear—just as readily as it translates into reality a thought driven by faith. What drives you most often? Fear or faith?

_____

_____

_____

_____

_____

_____

3

PUT YOUR SUBCONSCIOUS MIND TO WORK

utosuggestion is the medium for influencing the subconscious mind—a term that applies to all suggestions and all self-administered stimuli that reach a person's mind through the five senses (sight, hearing, smell, taste, touch). Stated another way, autosuggestion is self-suggestion. It is the agency of communication between that part of the mind where conscious thought takes place and serves as the seat of action for the subconscious mind.

Through the dominating thoughts that we permit to remain in our conscious mind (whether these thoughts are negative or positive is immaterial), the principle of auto-suggestion works to voluntarily influence the subconscious mind.

No thought, whether negative or positive, *can enter the subconscious mind without the aid of the principle of autosuggestion.* Otherwise stated, all impressions perceived through the five senses are stopped by the *conscious* thinking mind and may be either passed on to the subconscious mind or rejected. The conscious faculty serves as an outer guard to the approach of the subconscious.

Nature has built us so that we have *absolute control* over the material that reaches our subconscious minds through our five senses, although this is not meant to be construed as a statement that we always *exercise* this control. In the great majority of instances, we do *not* exercise it, which explains why so many people go through life in poverty and misery.

The subconscious mind resembles a fertile garden where weeds will grow in abundance if the seeds of more desirable crops are not sown. Autosuggestion is the agency of control through which an individual may voluntarily feed his or her subconscious mind on thoughts of a creative nature, or by neglect, permit thoughts of a destructive nature to find their way into this rich garden of the mind.

When you speak the object of your *desire* directly to your *subconscious* mind in a spirit of absolute *faith*, through repeating this procedure, you voluntarily create thought habits that are favorable to your efforts to transmute desire into its monetary equivalent.

The mere reading of the words is of no consequence unless you mix emotion or feeling with them—and reinforce success with declaring aloud your intent. For example, if you repeat a million times the famous Émile Coué formula, "Day by day, in every way, I am getting better and better," without mixing emotion and faith with your words, you will experience no desirable results. Your subconscious mind recognizes and acts upon *only* thoughts and declarations that have been well-mixed with emotion or feeling.

> **Your subconscious mind only recognizes and acts upon thoughts and declarations that have been well-mixed with emotion or feeling.**

This is a fact of such importance that it is repeated in practically every chapter of this book. The main reason that the majority of people who try to apply the principle of autosuggestion get no desirable results is because they don't understand that their subconscious minds only recognize and act upon thoughts and declarations that have been well-mixed with emotion or feeling.

Plain, unemotional words do not influence the subconscious mind. You will get no appreciable results until you learn to reach your subconscious mind with thoughts or spoken words that have been well-emotionalized with belief.

Do not become discouraged if you cannot control and direct your emotions the first time you try. Remember, there is no possibility to get something for nothing. The ability to reach and influence your subconscious mind has its price, which you must pay.

You cannot cheat, even if you desire to. The price of the ability to influence your subconscious mind is everlasting *persistence* in applying the principles in this book. *You alone* must decide whether or not the reward you are striving for (money/success consciousness) is worth the price you must pay for it in effort.

Wisdom and "cleverness" alone will not attract and retain wealth, except in a few very rare instances where the law of averages favors the attraction of success through these sources. The method of attracting money described in this book does not depend upon the law of averages.

Your ability to use the principle of autosuggestion will depend, very largely, upon your capacity to *concentrate* on a given *desire* until that desire becomes a burning obsession. When you begin to carry out the wisdom shared here, you need to tap into the power of *concentration*.

For example, when you "fix in your own mind the *exact* amount of money you desire," hold your thoughts on that amount of money by concentrating, or fixating your attention, with your eyes closed, until you can *actually see* the physical appearance of the money. Do this at least once each day. As you go through these exercises, *see yourself as actually in possession* of the money!

> **Your subconscious mind takes in and acts on all repeated orders given in a spirit of absolute faith.**

Here is a most significant fact–the subconscious mind takes any orders given it in a spirit of absolute *faith* and acts upon those orders. Know too that the orders often have to be presented over and over again, through repetition, before they are interpreted by the subconscious mind.

The following instructions are blended with the principles covered in this chapter, generating a condensed formula for transmuting desire into its monetary equivalent. Take these suggestions seriously and implement them as quickly as possible:

> **First.** Go to some quiet spot (preferably in bed at night) where you will not be disturbed or interrupted, close your eyes, and repeat aloud (so you can hear your own words) the written

statement of the amount of money you intend to accumulate, the time limit for its accumulation, and a description of the service or merchandise you intend to give in return for the money. As you carry out these instructions, see yourself as already in possession of the money.

For example, suppose you intend to accumulate $50,000 by the first of January, five years from now, by giving personal services as a salesperson in return for the money. Your written statement of your purpose should be similar to the following:

"By January 1, 20__, I will have in my possession $50,000 that will come to me in various amounts from time to time during the interim. In return for this money, I will give the most efficient service possible, rendering the fullest possible quantity and the best possible quality of service as a salesperson of (describe the service or merchandise you intend to sell).

"I believe that I will have this money in my possession. My faith is so strong that I can now see this money before my eyes. I can touch it with my hands. It is now awaiting transfer to me at the time and in the proportion that

I deliver the service I intend to provide in return for it. I am awaiting a plan by which to accumulate this money, and I will follow that plan when it is received."

Second. Repeat this program night and morning until you can see (in your imagination) the money you intend to accumulate.

Third. Place a written copy of your statement where you can see it at night and in the morning. Read it, aloud if possible, just before retiring and upon arising until you have it memorized.

Remember, as you carry out these instructions, you are applying the principle of autosuggestion for the purpose of giving orders to your subconscious mind. Remember also that your subconscious mind will act *only* upon instructions that are emotionalized and handed over to it with "feeling."

Faith is the strongest and most productive of the emotions. These instructions may at first seem abstract. Do not let this disturb you. The time will soon come, if you follow the directives in spirit as well as in action, that a whole new universe of power will unfold to you.

Skepticism, in connection will *all* new ideas, is characteristic of all human beings. But if you follow the instructions outlined here, your skepticism will soon be replaced by belief, and this, in turn, will soon become crystallized into *absolute faith.* Then you will have arrived at the point where you may truly say, "I am the master of my fate, I am the captain of my soul!"

THE SUBCONSCIOUS—THE CONNECTING LINK

The subconscious mind consists of a field of consciousness in which every impulse of thought that reaches the objective mind, through any of the five senses, is classified and recorded, and from which thoughts may be recalled or withdrawn, such as documents taken from a filing cabinet.

The subconscious mind receives and files sense impressions or thoughts, regardless of their nature. You may *voluntarily* plant in your subconscious mind any plan, thought, or purpose that you desire to translate into its physical or monetary equivalent. The subconscious acts first on the dominating desires that have been mixed with emotional feeling, such as faith.

The subconscious mind works day and night.

Through a method of procedure unknown to humankind, the subconscious mind draws on the forces of Infinite Intelligence for the power to voluntarily transmute someone's desires into their physical equivalent, making use always of the most practical media for its accomplishment.

You cannot entirely control your subconscious mind, but you can voluntarily hand over to it any plan, desire, or purpose to be transformed into concrete form.

There is plenty of evidence to support the belief that the subconscious mind is the connecting link between the finite mind of humans and Infinite Intelligence. It is the intermediary through which we can draw on the forces of Infinite Intelligence at will. It alone contains the secret process by which mental impulses are modified and changed into their spiritual equivalent. It alone is the medium through which prayer may be transmitted to the Source capable of answering prayer.

The possibilities of creative effort connected with the subconscious mind are stupendous and imponderable. They inspire us with awe.

I never approach the discussion of the subconscious mind without a feeling of littleness and inferiority due, perhaps, to the fact that our entire stock of knowledge on this subject is so pitifully limited. The very fact that the subconscious mind is the medium of communication between the thinking mind of humans and Infinite Intelligence is, of itself, a thought that almost paralyzes a person's reason.

After you have accepted as reality the existence of the sub-conscious mind and understand its possibilities as a medium for transmuting your desires into their physical or monetary equivalent, you will comprehend the full significance of the six steps detailed in Chapter 1. You will also understand why you have been repeatedly admonished to *make your desires clear and commit them to writing and declaration.* You will also understand the necessity of *persistence* in speaking out and carrying out instructions.

> # Control your mind so no undesirable thought will enter your subconscious mind.

The 11 principles, or steps, mentioned in Chapter 1 are the stimuli you acquire for the ability to reach and influence your subconscious mind. Do not become discouraged if you cannot do this on the first attempt. Remember that the sub-conscious mind may be voluntarily directed only through habit, using the instructions given in Chapter 1 on igniting your burning desire. You have not yet had time to master faith. Be patient. Be persistent.

A good many statements in the chapters on faith and autosuggestion will be repeated here, for the benefit of your subconscious mind. Remember, your subconscious mind functions voluntarily, whether you make any effort to influence it or not. This, naturally, suggests to you that thoughts of fear and poverty and all negative thoughts serve as stimuli to your subconscious mind–unless you master these impulses and give it more desirable food on which to feed.

The subconscious mind will not remain idle! *If you fail to plant desires* in your subconscious mind, it will feed on the thoughts that reach it as the result of your neglect. We have already explained that thought impulses, both negative and positive, are reaching the subconscious mind continuously.

For the present, it is sufficient if you remember that you are living daily in the midst of all manner of thought impulses that are reaching your subconscious mind without your knowledge. Some of these impulses are negative; some are positive. You are now engaged in trying to shut off the flow of negative impulses and purposely influencing your subconscious mind through positive impulses of constructive and deliberate desire.

When you achieve this, you will possess the key that unlocks the door to your subconscious mind. Moreover, you will control that door so completely that no undesirable thought will influence your subconscious mind.

> **Emotionalized thoughts have more—if not the only—action influence upon the subconscious mind.**

The subconscious mind is more susceptible to influence by impulses of thought mixed with "feeling" or emotion than by those originating solely in the reasoning portion of the mind. In fact, there is much evidence to support the theory that *only* emotionalized thoughts have any *action influence* on the subconscious mind. It is a well-known fact that emotion, or feeling, rules the majority of people.

If it is true that the subconscious mind responds more quickly to, and is influenced more readily by, thought impulses that are well mixed with emotion, then it is essential to become familiar with the more important of the emotions. There are seven major positive emotions and seven major negative emotions. The negatives voluntarily inject themselves into the thought impulses, which ensure passage into the subconscious mind. The positives must be injected, through the principle of autosuggestion, into the thought impulses that we want to pass on to our subconscious mind. Instructions for this have been given earlier in this chapter.

These emotions, or feeling impulses, may be likened to yeast in a loaf of bread, because they constitute the *action* element that transforms thought impulses from the passive to the active state. Thus we can understand why thought impulses, which have been well mixed with emotion, are acted upon more readily than thought impulses originating in "cold reason."

You are preparing yourself to influence and control the "inner audience" of your subconscious mind in order to hand over to it the desire for success, which you wish to be transmuted into its monetary equivalent. It is essential, therefore, that you understand the method of approach to this "inner audience." You must speak its language, or it will not heed your call. It understands best the language of emotion or feeling.

> **You must speak the language of your subconscious mind, or it will not listen.**

Let's examine the seven major positive emotions and the seven major negative emotions so that you may draw on the positives and avoid the negatives when giving instructions to your subconscious mind.

THE SEVEN MAJOR POSITIVE EMOTIONS

1. Desire

2. Faith

3. Love

4. Sex

5. Enthusiasm

6. Romance

7. Hope

There are other positive emotions, but these are the seven most powerful and the ones most commonly used in creative effort. Master these seven emotions (they can be mastered only by *use*), and the other positive emotions will be at your command when you need them. You are studying a book intended to help you develop a "money consciousness" by filling your mind with positive emotions. You will not become money conscious by filling your mind with negative emotions.

THE SEVEN MAJOR NEGATIVE EMOTIONS

1. Fear

2. Jealousy

3. Hatred

4. Revenge

5. Greed

6. Superstition

7. Anger

Positive and negative emotions cannot occupy the mind at the same time. One or the other must dominate. It is your responsibility to make sure that positive emotions constitute the dominating influence of your mind. Here the law of *habit* will come to your aid. Form the habit of applying and using positive emotions! Eventually, they will dominate your mind so completely that the negatives cannot enter.

Only by following these instructions literally and continuously can you gain control over your subconscious mind. The presence of a single negative in your conscious mind is sufficient to destroy all chances of constructive aid from your subconscious mind.

QUESTIONS TO CONSIDER

1. I can be the master of myself and my environment because I have the power to influence my subconscious mind. How able am I to control my mind, as well as my subconscious mind?

_____

_____

_____

_____

_____

2. I can't entirely control my subconscious mind, but I can voluntarily hand over to it any plan, desire, or purpose I want to transform into concrete form. How often do I do that?

_____

_____

_____

_____

_____

3. Of the seven major negative emotions, which two am I most susceptible to allowing space in my mind and my subconscious mind? What habit can I form to combat that tendency?

_____

_____

_____

_____

_____

_____

4. I know that my subconscious mind functions voluntarily, whether I make any effort to influence it or not. Negativity can infiltrate my mind as quickly as positivity—how quickly do I push out negative thoughts and replace with positive thoughts?

_____

_____

_____

_____

_____

_____

4

HARNESS YOUR IMAGINATION WITH GOALS

The imagination is literally the workshop where all plans are fashioned. An individual's impulse, or *desire*, is given shape, form, and *action* through the aid of the imaginative faculty of the mind.

It has been said that people can create anything they can imagine. Of all the ages of civilization, this is the most favorable for the development of the imagination because it is an age of rapid change. At every turn we encounter stimuli that develop the imagination.

Through the aid of our imaginative faculty, we have discovered and harnessed more of Nature's forces during the past 50 years than during the entire history of the human race. We have conquered the air so completely that the birds are a poor match for flying. We have harnessed the ether and made it serve as a means of instantaneous communication with any part of the world.

We have analyzed and weighed the sun at a distance of millions of miles and determined, through the aid of the *imagination*, the elements of which it consists. We have discovered that our brains are broadcasting and receiving stations for the vibration of thought. And we are beginning now to learn how to make practical use of this discovery.

> **The imaginative faculty consists of the synthetic imagination and the creative imagination.**

There are two modes in which the imaginative faculty operates: the "synthetic imagination" and the "creative imagination."

Synthetic imagination: Through the synthetic imagination, we can arrange old concepts, ideas, or plans into new combinations. This faculty creates nothing; it merely processes the material of experience, education, and observation with which it is fed to generate differently structured ideas. It is the faculty used most frequently by the inventor, with the exception of the "genius" who draws upon the creative imagination when he or she cannot solve a problem through the synthetic imagination.

Creative imagination: Through the faculty of the creative imagination, the finite mind of humans has direct communication with Infinite Intelligence. It is the faculty through which "hunches" and "inspirations" are received. It is by this faculty that all basic or new ideas are handed over to people.

> ## The creative imagination generates new ideas in collaboration with Infinite Intelligence.

The creative imagination works automatically in the manner described in subsequent pages. This faculty functions *only* when the conscious mind is vibrating at an exceedingly rapid rate–as, for example, when the conscious mind is stimulated through the emotion of a strong desire. The creative faculty becomes more alert, more receptive to vibrations from the sources mentioned, in proportion to its development through *use*. This statement is significant! Ponder over it before reading on.

Keep in mind as you follow these 11 steps, or principles, that the entire story will be complete only when you have *mastered, assimilated, and make use* of them all.

The great leaders of business, industry, finance, and the great artists, musicians, poets, and writers distinguished themselves because they developed the faculty of creative imagination. Both the synthetic and creative faculties of imagination become more alert with use, just as any muscle or organ of the body develops through use.

Desire is only a thought, an impulse. It is nebulous and ephemeral. It is abstract and of no value until it has been transformed into its physical counterpart. The synthetic imagination is the one used most frequently in the process of transforming the impulse of *desire* into money. But keep in mind that you may face circumstances and situations that demand use of the creative imagination as well.

Your imaginative faculty may have become weak through inaction. It can be revived and made alert through *use*. This faculty does not die, though it may become quiescent through lack of use.

Transformation of the *intangible impulse of desire into the tangible reality of money* calls for the use of a plan, or plans. These plans must be formed with the aid of the imagination—mainly, with the help of the synthetic imaginative faculty.

Begin at once to put your imagination to work on the building of a plan, or plans, for the transformation of your desire into money. Detailed instructions for the building of plans have been given in almost every chapter. Carry out the instructions best suited to your needs, and commit your plan to writing if you have not already done so. Then, speak it into reality!

> **Transforming an intangible desire into the tangible reality of money requires a plan.**

BE A GOAL SETTER

It is up to you to imagine and then decide what you want from life. When you decide, you can take possession of your mind and use it to reach goals of your own choosing. And you can literally accomplish anything—as long as it does not violate the laws of God or the rights of others. You can experience the thrill of knowing that you can achieve any goal or objective you set out to accomplish.

Setting goals is one way to keep your mind on the things you want, and off the things you don't want. You need to learn to set short- and long-term goals on a daily basis. This is very important. Write your goals on a sheet of paper. Visualize yourself achieving those goals. Constantly refer to them in an expectant, positive manner.

> ## You can experience the thrill of achieving any goal or objective you set out to accomplish.

I encourage you to set a goal right now. In doing so, follow the D-E-S-I-R-E formula:

- **Determine**
- **Evaluate**
- **Set a date**
- **Identify**
- **Repeat**
- **Each day**

Let's begin:

Determine: What do you want? Be definite.

Evaluate: What will you give in return?

Set a date: When will you have what you want?

Identify: Make a plan. What will you do at once?

Repeat: Repeat your step-by-step plan in writing. (You may need more space than is allowed here.)

Step 1. _____

Step 2. _____

Step 3. _____

Step 4. _____

Step 5. _____

Each day: Each and every day, morning and evening, read your written statement aloud–speak it into reality. Visualize yourself already in possession of your objective as you read.

Now that you set your goal, I encourage you to take this self-evaluation quiz to reveal some insight into your reasoning. Circle the answer that most closely reflects your view:

1. Which best describes your goals?

   a) Can't really describe them.

   b) Not getting fired, avoiding bankruptcy, not getting sick, minimizing conflict at home.

c) A clear plan for career advancement, definite financial targets, regular activity to increase your health, greater and deeper partnership with your spouse.

2. What are you doing to achieve your goals?

   a) Fantasizing about what life would be like.

   b) Struggling to avoid losing ground and dealing with any crisis as soon as it arises.

   c) Following a written plan, which I review daily, that outlines immediate, mid-range, and long-term steps.

3. What do you expect to give in return for achieving your goals?

   a) No idea.

   b) As little as possible, since it's been hard enough to get this far. I need to get rich quick.

   c) As much time, energy, devotion, service to my community, and whatever other specifics are required.

4. When did you last review your goals?

   a) Can't review them because they aren't set.

   b) In the midst of the last crisis.

   c) Today, as I do every day.

Nowhere is the weakness of a passive approach to life more evident than in the wheel-spinning that comes as a result of not setting goals. You can't get someplace you've never been before without planning your trip.

Any "a" answers to the questions should immediately alert you to why you are dissatisfied with your current situation in life.

How can you complain that things aren't to your liking if you don't know what it is you really want? The trap many people fall into is telling themselves that they do have goals—and then express all those goals in negative terms. As you have already learned, concentrating on what you don't want to happen almost ensures that it will happen. The first two "b" answers illustrate this kind of negative mental attitude.

You must acknowledge that even positively expressed goals are not achieved by wishing. You must take an active role in their execution, and be willing to return something for whatever you hope to gain.

Whether like Henry Ford you become immensely wealthy by providing automobiles to a nation, or like Henry Fonda you achieve great fame by offering extraordinary entertainment, you must give in order to get. This is the lesson of the third "b" response.

The fourth "b" response underscores the importance of staying focused on your goals. Every day you will make many decisions that can affect their possible realization. To do this best, you must regularly remind yourself of what your goals are so you can actively pursue them.

The "c" responses represent the focused approach to living that positive mental attitude (PMA) goal-setting provides. (Much more about PMA in Chapter 8.) You know and concentrate your thoughts on what you want. You have a plan for achieving your ambitions, and you review it often. In this way, all your actions and prayers move you forward toward a chosen, desired target or goal.

It is likely that at several points in your life you will consider changing your goals. Do not be distressed when this happens. We all gain wisdom and find opportunities we never dreamed existed. If you are aware of what you want, and you know from experience that you can pursue

it, you will be able to analyze these opportunities; and if you so choose, embrace them with confidence. That is the essence of having a positive mental attitude.

Bonus: Keep a slip of paper in your pocket or purse with your goals for the day written on it. It will be a reminder every time you reach for change or your keys. No pocket or purse? Then keep it where you will encounter it frequently during the day.

QUESTIONS TO CONSIDER

1. The thought impulse of desire is given shape, form, and action through the aid of the imaginative faculty of the mind. How imaginative are my desires?

_____

_____

_____

_____

2. If people can create anything they can imagine, what do I want to create?

_____

_____

_____

_____

_____

_____

_____

3. Of all the ages of civilization, this is the most favorable for the development of the imagination as it is a rapid-change era. Because my only limitation, within reason, lies in my development and use of my imagination, what is the wildest and most uncommon idea that comes to mind most often?

_____

_____

_____

_____

_____

4. Using my imagination to decide on a goal, I chose as my goal _____.

5. In the self-evaluation quiz, did you answer mostly a or b or c? What did you learn about yourself from the results?

_____

_____

_____

_____

_____

_____

5

YOUR DRIVING FORCE

The mastermind alliance may be defined as the "coordination of knowledge and effort, in a spirit of harmony between two or more people, for the attainment of a definite purpose." The mastermind alliance is your driving force.

In Chapter 1, you were instructed to take six concrete, practical steps as your first move in translating the desire for money into its physical equivalent. One of these steps is the formation of a *definite*, practical plan, or plans, through which this transformation may be made—including forming a mastermind group.

THE FOLLOWING ARE FOUR STEPS TO BUILD PRACTICAL PLANS THROUGH THE MECHANISM OF A MASTERMIND ALLIANCE:

1. *Ally yourself with a group* of as many people as you may need for the creation and carrying out of your plan(s) for the accumulation of money, or any other desire.

2. Before forming your mastermind alliance, decide what *advantages and benefits you may offer the individual members* of your group in return for their cooperation. No intelligent person will either request or expect another to work without adequate compensation, although this may not always be in the form of money.

3. Arrange to *meet with the members of your mastermind group* at least twice a week—more often if possible—until you have jointly perfected the necessary plan, or plans, for the accumulation of money, or the achievement of your goal.

4. Maintain *perfect harmony* between yourself and every member of your mastermind group. If you fail to carry out this instruction to the letter, you may meet with failure. The mastermind principle cannot obtain cohesion where perfect harmony does not prevail.

To have great power, you must avail yourself of the mastermind principle. In a preceding chapter, instructions were given for the creation of *plans* for the purpose of translating *desire* into its monetary equivalent. If you carry out these instructions with *persistence* and intelligence and use discrimination in the selection of your mastermind group, your objective will have been halfway reached even before you begin to recognize it.

There are two characteristics of the mastermind principle: ECONOMIC and PSYCHIC.

So that you may better understand the "intangible" potentialities of power available to you through a properly chosen mastermind group, we will here explain the two characteristics of the mastermind principle, one of which is *economic* in nature and the other *psychic*.

The *economic* feature is obvious. Economic advantages may be created by people who surround themselves with the advice, counsel, and personal cooperation of a group willing to lend you wholehearted aid in a spirit of *perfect harmony.* This form of cooperative alliance has been the basis of nearly every great fortune. Your understanding of this great truth may definitely determine your financial status.

The *psychic* aspect to the mastermind principle is much more abstract, much more difficult to comprehend, because it references spiritual forces with which the human race as a whole is not well acquainted. You may catch a significant suggestion from this statement: "No two minds ever come together without, thereby, creating a third, invisible, intangible force which may be likened to a third mind."

Keep in mind the fact that there are only two known elements in the whole universe—energy and matter. It is a well-known fact that matter may be broken down into units of molecules, atoms, and electrons. There are units of matter that may be isolated, separated, and analyzed.

Likewise, there are units of energy.

The human mind is a form of energy, a part of it being spiritual in nature. When the minds of two people are coordinated in a *spirit of harmony*, the spiritual units of energy of each mind form an affinity, which constitutes the psychic dimension of the mastermind.

The mastermind principle, or rather the economic feature of it, was first called to my attention by one of the riches Americans in history, Andrew Carnegie. Discovery of this principle was responsible for the choice of my life's work.

> **Great power and success can be accumulated with the mastermind principle.**

Mr. Carnegie's mastermind group consisted of approximately fifty men with whom he surrounded himself for the *definite purpose* of manufacturing and marketing steel. He attributed his entire fortune to the *power* he accumulated through this mastermind.

Analyze the record of anyone who has accumulated a great fortune and many of those who have accumulated modest fortunes, and you will find that they have either consciously or unconsciously employed the mastermind principle.

> **People take on the nature, habits, and power of thought of those with whom they associate in a spirit of sympathy and harmony.**

Energy is Nature's universal building block, out of which is constructed every material thing in the universe, including humankind, and every form of animal and vegetable life. Through a process that only Nature completely understands, energy is translated into matter.

Nature's building blocks are available to humankind in the energy involved in *thinking*! Your brain can be compared to an electric battery. It absorbs energy from the ether, which permeates every atom of matter and fills the entire universe.

It is a well-known fact that a group of electric batteries will provide more energy than a single battery. It is also a well-known fact that an individual battery will provide energy in proportion to the number and capacity of the cells it contains.

The brain functions in a similar fashion. This accounts for the fact that some brains are more efficient than others, and it leads to this significant statement: a group of brains coordinated (or connected) in a spirit of harmony will provide more thought-energy than a single brain, just as a group of electric batteries will provide more energy than a single battery.

Through this metaphor it becomes immediately obvious that the mastermind principle holds the secret of the *power* wielded by people who surround themselves with other people of brains.

There follows, now, another statement that will lead still nearer to an understanding of the psychic dimension of the mastermind principle: when a group of individual brains are coordinated and function in harmony, the increased energy created through that alliance becomes available to every individual brain in the group.

Henry Ford whipped poverty, illiteracy, and ignorance by allying himself with great minds. Through his association with Edison, Burbank, Burroughs, and Firestone, Mr. Ford added to his own brainpower the sum and substance of the intelligence, experience, knowledge, and spiritual forces of these four men. Moreover, he appropriated and made use of the mastermind principle through the methods described in this book. *This principle is available to you!*

> # Power, or organized effort, is produced through the coordination of effort in a mastermind alliance.

Because *power* is essential for success in the accumulation of money, *plans* are inert and useless without sufficient *power* to translate them into *action*. And because *power* is defined as "organized and intelligently directed knowledge," it is important to examine the sources of knowledge–then put that *knowledge into action*:

- **Infinite Intelligence.** This source of knowledge is absorbed with the aid of creative imagination.

- **Accumulated experience.** The accumulated experience of a person (or that portion of it that has been organized and recorded), may be found in any well-equipped public library and from credible sources on the Internet. An important part of this accumulated experience is taught in public schools and colleges, where it has been classified and organized.

- **Experiment and research.** In the field of science, and in practically every other walk of life, people are gathering, classifying, and organizing new facts daily. This is the source to turn to when knowledge is not available through "accumulated experience." Here, too, the creative imagination must often be used.

Knowledge may be acquired from any of these three sources and converted into *power* by organizing it into definite *plans* and by expressing those plans in terms of *action*.

Examination of these three major sources of knowledge will readily disclose the difficulty you may have if dependent on your efforts alone in assembling knowledge and expressing it through definite plans in terms of action. If your plans are comprehensive, and if they contemplate large proportions, you must induce others to cooperate before you can inject into them the necessary element of power.

> **People take on the nature, habits, and power of thought of those with whom they associate in a spirit of sympathy and harmony.**

Power is "organized and intelligently directed knowledge," and it is produced through the coordination of effort of two or more people, working together in a spirit of harmony toward a definite goal.

GROUP SPEAK

You have learned that everything humankind creates or acquires begins in the form of *desire* and that desire is taken on the first lap of its journey, from the abstract to the concrete, through the workshop of the *imagination*, where *plans* for its transition are created and organized.

> ## Organized planning is the crystallization of DESIRE into ACTION.

Keep in mind these two facts:

First. You are engaged in an undertaking of major importance to you. To be sure of success, you must have faultless plans.

Second. You must have the advantage of the experience, education, native ability, and imagination of other minds. This is in harmony with the methods followed by every person who has accumulated a great fortune.

No individual has sufficient experience, education, native ability, and knowledge to ensure the accumulation of a great fortune without the cooperation of other people. Every plan you adopt in your endeavor to accumulate wealth should be the joint creation of yours and every member of your mastermind group. You may originate your own plans, either in whole or in part, but *ensure that your plans are reviewed and approved by the members of your mastermind alliance.*

> **No individual has sufficient experience, education, native ability, and knowledge to ensure the accumulation of a great fortune without the cooperation of other people.**

If the first plan you adopt does not work successfully, replace it with a new plan; if this new plan fails to work, replace it; in turn with still another, and so on, *until you find a plan that does work.* Right here is the point at which the majority of people meet with failure–their lack of *persistence* to create new plans to take the place of those that fail.

> **Your achievements can be no greater than your plans are sound.**

Henry Ford accumulated a fortune not because of his superior mind, but because he adopted and followed a *sound plan*. A thousand people could be pointed out as having a better education than Ford's, yet those thousand live in poverty because they do not possess the right plan for the accumulation of money, or the right plan for the desired lifestyle.

The most intelligent person living cannot succeed in accumulating money—nor in any other undertaking—without practical and workable plans. Keep this fact in mind when your plans fail: *temporary defeat is not permanent failure*. It may only mean that your plans have not been sound. Build other plans. Start all over again.

> # Temporary defeat is not permanent failure.

Edison "failed" ten thousand times before he perfected the incandescent electric light bulb. That means, he met with temporary defeat ten thousand times before his efforts were crowned with success.

Temporary defeat should mean only one thing: the certain knowledge that there is something wrong with your plan. Millions of people go through life in misery and poverty because they lack a sound plan through which to acquire happiness and a fortune.

> ## There are two types of people in the world: LEADERS and FOLLOWERS. Decide at the outset which you intend to be.

The following are important, major attributes of leadership:

1. **Unwavering courage** based on knowledge of self and your occupation. No follower wishes to be dominated by a leader who lacks self-confidence and courage. No intelligent follower will be dominated by such a leader very long.

2. **Self-control.** People who cannot control themselves can never control others. Self-control sets

a mighty example for your followers, which the more intelligent will emulate.

3. **A keen sense of justice.** Without a sense of fairness and justice, no leader can command and retain the respect of the followers.

4. **Definiteness of decision.** Those who waver in decisions show that they are not sure of themselves. They cannot lead others successfully.

5. **Definiteness of plans.** Successful leaders must plan their work and work their plan. Leaders who move by guesswork, without practical, definite plans, is comparable to a ship without a rudder. Sooner or later they will land on the rocks.

6. **The habit of doing more than one is paid for doing.** One of the penalties of leadership is the necessity of willingness, on the part of the leader, to do more than is required of the followers.

7. **A pleasing personality.** No slovenly, careless person can become a successful leader. Leadership calls for respect. Followers will not respect a leader who does not grade high on all the factors of a pleasing personality.

8. **Sympathy and understanding.** The successful leader must be in sympathy with the followers.

Moreover, good leaders must understand them and their problems.

9. **Mastery of detail.** Successful leadership calls for mastery of details of the leader's position.

10. **Willingness to assume full responsibility.** The successful leader must be willing to assume responsibility for the mistakes and the short-comings of the followers. If a leader tries to shift this responsibility, he or she will not remain the leader. If one of the followers makes a mistake and is shown to be incompetent, the leader must accept that as a failure for hiring such a person.

11. **Cooperation.** The successful leader must under-stand and apply the principle of cooperative effort and be able to induce the followers to do the same. *Leadership calls for power, and power calls for cooperation.*

It is just as essential to know what not to do as it is to know what to do.

There are ten major causes of failure in leadership:

1. **Inability to organize details.** Efficient leadership calls for the ability to organize and master details. No genuine leader is ever "too busy" to do anything required in his or her capacity as the leader. Whether you are a leader or a follower, when you admit you are "too busy" to change your plan or give attention to an emergency, you admit inefficiency. The successful leader must be the master of all details connected with the position. That means, of course, acquiring the habit of delegating tasks to capable colleagues.

2. **Unwillingness to render humble service.** Truly great leaders are willing, when the occasion demands, to perform any sort of labor they would ask someone else to perform.

3. **Expectation of pay for what they "know" instead of what they "do" with what they know.** The world does not pay people for what they *know*. It pays them for what they *do*, or induce others to do.

4. **Fear of competition from followers.** The leader who fears that one of the followers wants his or her position is practically sure to realize that fear

sooner or later. On the other hand, the able leader trains understudies and delegates tasks. Only in this way may a leader multiply and prepare to be at many places, giving attention to many things at one time. It is an eternal truth that people receive more pay for their *ability to get others to perform* than they could possibly earn by their own efforts. An efficient leader may, through knowledge of the job and the magnetism of personality, greatly increase the efficiency of others and induce them to render more and better service than they could render without his or her aid.

5. **Lack of imagination.** Without imagination, the leader is incapable of meeting emergencies and creating plans to guide the followers efficiently.

6. **Selfishness.** The leader who claims all the honor for the work of the team is sure to be met with resentment. The really great leader claims none of the honors. He or she is content to see the honors, when there are any, go to the followers, knowing that most people work harder for commendation and recognition than they will for money alone.

7. **Intemperance.** Followers do not respect an intemperate (overindulgent) leader. Moreover,

intemperance in any of its various forms destroys the endurance and vitality of all who indulge in it.

8. **Disloyalty.** Perhaps disloyalty should have been placed at the head of the list. The leader who is not loyal or trustworthy to associates—both those above and those below—cannot long maintain leadership. Disloyalty marks a person as contemptable. Lack of loyalty is one of the major causes of failure in every walk of life.

9. **Emphasis of the "authority" of leadership.** The efficient leader leads by encouraging, not by trying to instill fear in the hearts of the followers. The leader who tries to impress followers with "authority" is placed within the category of "leadership through force." If a leader is a real leader, he will have no need to advertise that fact except by good conduct—sympathy, understanding, fairness, and a demonstration that he or she knows the job.

10. **Emphasis of title.** The competent leader requires no "title" to gain the respect of followers. The leader who makes too much over a title generally has little else to emphasize. The doors to the office of the real leader are open to all who wish to enter, and his or her working quarters are free from formality or ostentation.

There are ten major causes of failure in leadership: inability to organize details, unwillingness to render humble service, expectation of pay for what they "know" instead of what they *do* with what they know, fear of competition from followers, lack of imagination, selfishness, intemperance, disloyalty, emphasis on the "authority" of leadership, and emphasis of title. Any one of these faults is sufficient to induce failure.

QUESTIONS TO CONSIDER

1. To establish a mastermind group I need to identify individuals whose experience, education, native ability, and imagination complement (not replicate) my own assets; determining what I will offer them in exchange for their cooperation; meeting regularly–at least twice per week; and ensuring that perfect harmony obtains in the group. Who comes to mind?

   _____

   _____

   _____

2. If the first plan I adopt does not work successfully, I need to replace it with a new plan; keep replacing it until I find one that works. Am I willing to face that cycle if need be? _____

3. The most intelligent person living cannot succeed in accumulating money–nor in any other undertaking– without practical and workable plans. I realize that my achievements can be no greater than my plans are sound. How solid are my plans? Do I need to revise them? Start over?

_____

_____

_____

_____

_____

4. Millions of people go through life in misery and poverty because they lack a sound plan through which to accumulate a fortune. I, though, am going to write a plan and share it with my mastermind alliance. And from there I will use my leadership skills to draw out the best in the group to accomplish our objective. What will I promise them in return?

_____

_____

_____

_____

_____

6

FOIL FAILURE

Accurate analysis of more than 25,000 men and women who had experienced failure disclosed the fact that *lack of decision* was near the top of the list of the thirty major causes of *failure*. This is no mere statement of a theory; it is a fact.

Procrastination, the opposite of *decision*, is a common enemy that almost every human being must conquer.

You will have an opportunity to test your capacity to reach quick and definite *decisions* when you finish reading this book and are ready to put into *action* the principles you learned.

> **Make a habit of reaching decisions quickly and definitely, and changing them slowly.**

Analysis of several hundred people who had accumulated fortunes well beyond the million-dollar mark disclosed the fact that every one of them had the habit of *reaching decisions promptly* and changing those decisions *slowly*, if and when they needed to be changed.

People who *fail* to accumulate money, without exception, have the habit of reaching decisions, *if at all,* very slowly, and of changing those decisions quickly and often.

One of Henry Ford's most outstanding qualities was his habit of reaching decisions quickly and definitely and changing them slowly. This quality was so pronounced in Mr. Ford that it gave him the reputation of being obstinate. However, it was this trait that prompted Mr. Ford to continue to manufacture his famous Model "T" when all of his advisors, and many of the purchasers of the car, were urging him to change it.

Perhaps, Mr. Ford delayed too long in making the change, but the other side of the story is that Mr. Ford's firmness of decision yielded a huge fortune, before the change in model became necessary. There is little doubt that Mr. Ford's habit of definiteness of decision assumes the proportion of obstinacy, but this quality is preferable to slowness in reaching decisions and quickness in changing them.

The majority of people who fail to accumulate money sufficient for their needs are generally easily influenced by the "opinions" of others. They permit newspapers and "gossiping" neighbors to do their "thinking" for them. Opinions are the cheapest commodities on earth. Everyone has a flock of opinions ready to be wished upon anyone who will accept them. If you are influenced by opinions when you reach decisions, you will not succeed in any undertaking, much less in that of transmuting your own desire into money.

> **If you are influenced by the opinions of others, you will have no desire of your own.**

When you begin to put into practice the principles described here, reach your own decisions and follow them. Take no one into your confidence, except the members of your mastermind group; and be very sure in your selection of this group that you choose only those who will be in complete agreement and harmony with your purpose.

Close friends and relatives, while not meaning to do so, often hinder someone with unsolicited opinions and sometimes ridicule, even if meant in jest. Thousands of men and women carry inferiority complexes with them all through life because some well-meaning but ignorant person destroyed their confidence through opinions or ridicule.

You have a brain and mind of your own. *Use it* to reach your own decisions. If you need facts or information from other people to enable you to reach decisions, as you probably will in many instances, acquire these facts or secure the information you need quietly, without disclosing your purpose.

It is characteristic of people who have only a smattering or a veneer of knowledge to try to give the impression that they have much knowledge. Such people generally do *too much talking and too little listening.* Keep your eyes and ears wide open—and your mouth closed—if you wish to acquire the habit of prompt decision-making. Those who talk too much do little else. If you talk more than you listen, you not only deprive yourself of many opportunities to accumulate useful knowledge, but you also disclose your *plans and purposes* to people who will take great delight in defeating you because they envy you.

> **The value of decisions depends upon the courage required to render them.**

The great decisions, which served as the foundation of civilization, were reached by assuming great risks, which often meant the possibility of death.

Abraham Lincoln's decision to issue his famous Emancipation Proclamation was rendered with full understanding that his act would turn thousands of friends and political supporters against him. He knew, too, that the carrying out of that proclamation would mean death to thousands of men on the battlefield. In the end, it cost Lincoln his life. That required courage.

Socrates' decision to drink the cup of poison rather than compromise in his personal belief was a decision of courage. It turned time ahead a thousand years and gave to people then unborn the right to freedom of thought and speech.

But the greatest decision of all time, as far as any American citizen is concerned, was reached in Philadelphia on July 4, 1776, when fifty-six men signed their names to a document that they well knew would either bring freedom to all Americans or leave every one of the fifty-six hanging from the gallows!

Analyze the events that led to the Declaration of Independence and you will be convinced that this nation, which now holds a position commanding respect and power among all nations of the world, was born of a *decision* created by a mastermind group consisting of fifty-six men.

Note the fact that it was their *decision* that ensured the success of George Washington's armies, because the spirit of that decision was in the heart of every soldier who fought with him and served as a spiritual power that recognizes no such thing as failure.

Note also (with great personal benefit) that the power that gave this nation its freedom is the self-same power that must be used by every individual who becomes self-determining. This power is made up of the principles described in this book. It is not difficult to detect in the story of the Declaration of Independence at least six of these principles: *desire, decision, faith, persistence, the mastermind,* and *organized planning.*

Throughout this philosophy is found the suggestion that *thought,* backed by strong *desire,* has a tendency to transmute itself into its physical equivalent. Before going further, I wish to leave with you the suggestion that you may find in the story of America's establishment a perfect description of the method by which thought makes this astounding transformation.

But in your search for the secret of the method, do not look for a miracle, because you will not find it. You will find only the eternal laws of Nature. These laws are available to every person who has the *faith* and *courage* to use them. They may be used to bring freedom to a nation or to accumulate riches. There is no charge except the time necessary to understand and appropriate them.

Those who reach decisions promptly and definitely know what they want and generally get it. Leaders in every walk of life decide quickly and firmly. That is the major reason why they are leaders. The world has the habit of making room for those whose words and actions show they know where they are going.

> ## Those who reach decisions promptly and definitely generally get what they want.

Indecision is a habit that usually begins when a person is young. The habit takes on permanency as the youth goes through grade school, high school, and even through college, without definiteness of purpose. The major weakness of all educational systems is that they neither teach nor encourage the habit of definite decision.

It would be beneficial if no college would permit the enrollment of any student unless and until the student declared his or her major purpose in matriculating. It would be of still greater benefit if every student who enters school were compelled to accept training in the habit of decision-making and forced to pass a satisfactory examination on this subject before being permitted to advance.

The habit of indecision, acquired because of the deficiencies in our school systems, goes with the student into the occupation chosen—if in fact an occupation is chosen. Generally, the youth just out of school seeks any job, taking the first one found. I venture to say that ninety-eight out of every hundred people working for wages today are in the positions they hold because they lacked the definiteness of decision to plan a definite position and the knowledge of how to choose an employer.

Definiteness of decision always requires courage—sometimes very great courage. The fifty-six men who signed the Declaration of Independence staked their lives on the decision to affix their signatures to that document. The person who reaches a definite decision to procure a particular job and make life pay the price asked does not stake his or her life on that decision; the decision is staked on *economic freedom*.

Financial independence, riches, and desirable professional positions are not within reach of the person who neglects or refuses to *expect, plan, and demand* these things. The person who desires riches in the same spirit that Samuel Adams desired freedom for the colonies is sure to accumulate wealth.

How many of the thirty causes of failure are holding you back?

Let's look at each one:

1. **Unfavorable heredity background.** There is little, if anything, that can be done for people who are born with a deficiency in brain power. This philosophy offers one method of bridging this weakness–through the aid of the mastermind. Observe with profit, however, that this is the *only* one of the thirty causes of failure that may not be easily corrected by any individual.

2. **Lack of a well-defined purpose in life.** There is no hope of success for the person who does not have a central purpose or definite goal at which to aim. Ninety-eight out of every hundred analyzed had no such aim. Perhaps this was the major cause of their failure.

3. **Lack of ambition to aim above mediocrity.** We offer no hope for the person who is so indifferent that he or she does not want to get ahead in life and is not willing to pay the price.

4. **Insufficient education.** This limitation may be overcome with comparative ease. Experience has proven that the best-educated people are often those who are known as "self-made" or self-educated. It takes more than a college degree to make an educated person. Anyone who is educated has learned to get whatever he or she wants in life without violating the rights

of others. Education consists, not so much of knowledge, but of knowledge effectively and persistently applied. People are paid not merely for what they know, but more particularly for what they do with what they know.

5. **Lack of self-discipline.** Discipline comes through self-control. This means that you must control all negative qualities. Before you can control conditions, you must first control yourself. Self-mastery is the hardest job you will ever tackle. If you do not conquer self, you will be conquered by self. You may see at one and the same time both your best friend and your greatest enemy by stepping in front of a mirror.

6. **Ill health.** No person may enjoy outstanding success without good health. Many of the causes of ill health are subject to mastery and control. These, in the main, are:

- overeating
- wrong habits of thought; giving expression to negatives
- wrong use of and over indulgence in sex
- lack of proper physical exercise.
- an inadequate supply of fresh air, due to improper breathing

7. **Unfavorable environmental influences during childhood.** "As the twig is bent, so shall the tree grow." Most people who have criminal tendencies acquire them as the result of a bad environment and improper associations during childhood.

8. **Procrastination.** Procrastination is one of the most common causes of failure. "Old Man Procrastination" stands within the shadow of every human being, awaiting his opportunity to spoil your chances of success. Most of us go through life as failures because we are waiting for the "time to be right" to start doing something worthwhile. Do not wait. The time will never be "just right." Start where you stand, and work with whatever tools you may have at your command; better tools will be found as you go along.

9. **Lack of persistence.** Most of us are good "starters" but poor "finishers" of everything we begin. Moreover, people are prone to give up at the first signs of defeat. There is no substitute for persistence. The person who makes persistence his or her watchword discovers that "Old Man Failure" finally becomes tired and departs. Failure cannot cope with persistence.

10. **Negative personality.** There is no hope of success for the person who repels people with a

negative personality. Success comes through the application of power, and power is attained through the cooperative efforts of other people. A negative personality will not induce cooperation.

11. **Lack of controlled sexual urge.** Sexual energy is the most powerful of all the stimuli that move people into action. Because it is the most powerful of the emotions, it must be controlled, through transmutation, and converted into other channels.

12. **Uncontrolled desire for "something for nothing."** The gambling instinct drives millions of people to failure. Evidence of this may be found in a variety of current events as well as a study of the Wall Street crash of 1929, during which millions of people tried to make money by gambling on stock margins.

13. **Lack of a well-defined power of decision.** People who succeed reach decisions promptly and change them, if at all, very slowly. People who fail reach decisions, if at all, very slowly and change them frequently and quickly. Indecision and procrastination are twins. Where one is found, the other is usually present. Kill off this pair before they completely hog-tie you to the treadmill of failure.

14. **One or more of the six basic fears.** These fears have been analyzed for you in Chapter 9. They must be mastered before you can market your services effectively.

15. **Wrong selection of a marriage partner.** This is one of the most common causes of failure. The relationship of marriage brings people intimately into contact. Unless this relationship is harmonious, failure is likely to follow. Moreover, it will be a form of failure marked by misery and unhappiness, destroying all signs of ambition.

16. **Overcaution.** The person who takes no chances generally has to take whatever is left when others are through choosing. Overcaution is as bad as under-caution. Both are extremes to be guarded against. Life itself is filled with the element of chance.

17. **Wrong selection of business associates.** This is one of the most common causes of failure in business. In marketing personal services, you should use great care to select an employer who will be an inspiration and who is intelligent and successful. We emulate those with whom we associate most closely. Pick an employer worth emulating.

18. **Superstition and prejudice.** Superstition is a form of fear. It is also a sign of ignorance. People who succeed keep open minds and are afraid of nothing.

19. **Wrong selection of vocation.** No one can succeed in an endeavor that they dislike. The most essential step in the marketing of personal services is that of selecting an occupation into which you can throw yourself wholeheartedly.

20. **Lack of concentration of effort.** The "jack-of-all-trades" seldom is good at any. Concentrate all your efforts on *one definite chief aim.*

21. **The habit of indiscriminate spending.** The spendthrift cannot succeed, mainly because he or she stands eternally in fear of poverty. Form the habit of systematic saving by putting aside a definite percentage of your income. Money in the bank gives you a very safe foundation of courage when bargaining for the sale of personal services. Without money, you must take what one is offered and be glad to get it.

22. **Lack of enthusiasm.** Without enthusiasm, you cannot be convincing. Moreover, enthusiasm is contagious, and the person who possesses it in a controlled form is generally welcome in any group of people.

23. **Intolerance.** The person with a "closed" mind on any subject seldom gets ahead. Intolerance means that the person has stopped acquiring knowledge. The most damaging forms of intolerance are those connected with religious, racial, and political differences of opinion.

24. **Intemperance.** The most damaging forms of intemperance are connected with eating, strong drink, and sexual activities. Overindulgence in any of these is fatal to success.

25. **Inability to cooperate with others.** More people lose their positions and their big opportunities in life because of the inability to cooperate than for all other reasons combined. It is a fault that no well-informed business person or leader will tolerate.

26. **Possession of power that was not acquired through self-effort** (sons and daughters of wealthy parents and others who inherit money that they did not earn). Power in the hands of someone who did not acquire it gradually is often fatal to success. Quick riches are more dangerous than poverty.

27. **Intentional dishonesty.** There is no substitute for honesty. Someone may be temporarily dishonest by force of circumstances over which he

or she has no control without permanent damage. But there is no hope for the person who is dishonest by choice. Sooner or later, the deeds will catch up and the person will pay by loss of reputation, and perhaps even loss of liberty.

28. **Egotism and vanity.** These two qualities serve as red lights that warn others to keep away. They are fatal to success.

29. **Guessing instead of thinking.** Most people are too indifferent or lazy to acquire facts with which to think accurately. They prefer to act on opinions created by guesswork or snap judgments.

30. **Lack of capital.** This is a common cause of failure among those who start out in business for the first time without sufficient reserve of capital to absorb the shock of their mistakes and to carry them over until they have established a reputation.

QUESTIONS TO CONSIDER

1. Procrastination is a common enemy that everyone must conquer. Analysis of several hundred millionaires showed that each one had the habit of making decisions promptly and changing them slowly, if at all. Am I a procrastinator or a decisionmaker?

2. The majority of people who fail to accumulate money sufficient for their needs are generally easily influenced by the opinions of others. Everyone willingly shares their opinions with anyone willing to listen. Am I swayed too much by what other people think, believe, feel?

3. The value of good decisions often depends on courage. Am I courageous enough to plan, make wise decisions promptly, foil failure, establish a mastermind alliance, and speak my goals and desires into reality?

_____

_____

_____

_____

_____

_____

_____

_____

_____

_____

_____

4. Which five of the thirty major causes of failure stands between me and success?

_____

_____

_____

_____

7

PERSONALIZE YOUR BROADCASTING STATION

When working in conjunction with the late Dr. Alexander Graham Bell and Dr. Elmer R. Gates, I observed that every human brain is both a broadcasting and receiving station for the vibration of thought.

Through the medium of the ether, in a fashion similar to that employed by the radio broadcasting principle, every human brain is capable of picking up vibrations of thought that are being released by other brains.

In connection with the statement in the preceding paragraph, compare and consider the description of the creative imagination, as outlined in Chapter 4. The creative imagination is the "receiving set" of the brain. It is the agency of communication between our conscious, or reasoning mind, and the four sources from which we may receive thought stimuli. The subconscious mind is the "sending station" of the brain, through which vibrations of thought are broadcast.

> # Your brain is the broadcasting and receiving station for thought.

When stimulated, or "stepped up" to a high rate of vibration, the mind becomes more receptive to the vibration of thought that reaches it through the ether from outside sources. This "stepping up" process takes place through positive or negative emotions. Through the emotions, the vibrations of thought may be increased.

Vibrations of an exceedingly high rate are the only vibrations picked up and carried by the ether from one brain to another. Thought is energy traveling at an exceedingly high rate of vibration. Thought, which has been modified or "stepped up" by any of the major emotions, vibrates at a much higher rate than ordinary thought, and it is this type of thought that passes from one brain to another, through the broadcasting machinery of the human brain.

> ## Thought is energy traveling at an exceedingly high rate of vibration.

The emotion of sex stands at the head of the list of human emotions, as far as intensity and driving force are concerned. The brain stimulated by the emotion of sex vibrates at a much more rapid rate than it does when that emotion is quiescent or absent.

The result of sex transmutation is the increase of the rate of vibration of thoughts to such a pitch that the creative imagination becomes highly receptive to ideas, which it picks up from the ether. On the other hand, when the brain is vibrating at a rapid rate, it not only attracts thoughts and ideas released by other brains through the medium of the ether, but it gives to our own thoughts that "feeling" that is essential before those thoughts will be picked up and acted on by our subconscious mind.

Thus, you will see that the broadcasting principle is the factor through which you mix feeling, or emotion, with your thoughts and pass them on to your subconscious mind.

Along with the important factors of the subconscious mind and the faculty of the creative imagination, which constitute the sending and receiving sets of your mental broadcasting machinery, consider now the principle of auto-suggestion, which is the medium by which you may put into operation your "broadcasting" station.

Through the instructions described in Chapter 1, you were informed of the method by which desire may be transmuted into its monetary equivalent.

Operation of your mental "broadcasting" station is a comparatively simple procedure. You have three principles to bear in mind and apply when you wish to use your broadcasting station: 1) the subconscious mind, 2) the creative imagination, and 3) autosuggestion. The stimuli through which you put these three principles into action have been described; the procedure begins with desire.

> When you wish to use your broadcasting station, you have three principles to bear in mind and apply:
>
> the SUBCONSCIOUS MIND, the CREATIVE IMAGINATION, and AUTOSUGGESTION.

If you understand the principle described in Chapter 5 on the mastermind alliance, you of course recognize the roundtable procedure here described as being a practical application of the mastermind. This method of mind stimulation, through harmonious discussion of definite subjects between three people, illustrates the simplest and most practical use of the mastermind.

By adopting and following a similar plan, any student of this philosophy may come into possession of the famous Carnegie formula briefly described in previous chapters.

Inventory yourself.

Before you can put any portion of this philosophy into successful use, your mind must be prepared to receive it. The preparation is not difficult. It begins with study, analysis, and understanding of three enemies that you have to clear out of your mind: *indecision, doubt,* and *fear!*

Your sixth sense will never function while these three negatives, or any one of them, remain in your mind. The members of this unholy trio are closely related; where one is found, the other two are close at hand.

Indecision is the seedling of fear! Remember that indecision crystallizes into doubt; the two blend and become fear! The "blending" process often is slow. This is one reason why these three enemies are so dangerous. They germinate and grow without their presence being observed.

The purpose of this chapter is to turn the spotlight on the cause and the cure of the six basic fears. Before we can master an enemy, we must know its name, its habits, and its place of abode. As you read, analyze yourself carefully and determine which, if any, of the six common fears have attached to you.

Do not be deceived by the habits of these subtle enemies. Sometimes they remain hidden in the subconscious mind, where they are difficult to locate and still more difficult to eliminate.

Fear is nothing more than a state of mind.

There are six basic fears that every human suffers from at one time or another. Most people are fortunate if they do not suffer from the entire six. Named in the order of their most common appearance, they are the fears of:

1. Poverty

2. Criticism

3. Ill health

4. Loss of someone's love

5. Old age

6. Death

All other fears are of minor importance and can be grouped under these six headings.

The prevalence of these fears, as a curse to the world, runs in cycles. For almost six years, during the Great Depression, many floundered in the cycle of the fear of poverty. During the world wars, many lived in the cycle of the fear of death. Following wars, many live in the cycle of the fear of ill health, evidenced by the epidemic of diseases worldwide.

Fears are nothing more than states of mind. Our states of mind are subject to control and direction. Through the principles detailed in this book, you may control your thoughts and master your fears so that you translate thoughts of abundance into physical reality, rather than destructive thought impulses born of fear.

Remember: humans can create nothing that they do not first conceive in the form of an impulse of thought. Following this statement comes another of still greater importance:

Our thought impulses begin immediately to translate into a physical equivalent, whether those thoughts are voluntary or involuntary. Thought impulses picked up by mere chance (thoughts that have been released by other minds) may determine your financial, business, professional, or social destiny just as surely as do the thought impulses that we create by intent and design.

We are here laying the foundation for the presentation of a fact of great importance to the person who does not understand why some people appear to be "lucky" while others of equal or greater ability, training, experience, and brain capacity seem destined to ride with misfortune. This fact may be explained by the statement that *every human being has the ability to completely control their own minds; and with this control, obviously, every person may open their minds to the negative thought impulses being released by other brains, or close the doors tightly and admit only thought impulses of their own choice.*

Nature has endowed us with absolute control over only one thing: thought. This fact, coupled with the additional fact that everything that we create begins in the form of a thought, leads us very near to the principle by which fear may be mastered.

If it is true that *all thought has a tendency to clothe itself in its physical equivalent* (this is true beyond any reasonable room for doubt), it is equally true that thought impulses of fear and poverty cannot be translated into terms of courage and financial gain.

The six basic fears become translated into a state of worry through indecision. Take these steps to overcome fears:

- Relieve yourself forever of the fear of death by deciding to accept death as an inescapable event.

- Whip the fear of poverty by reaching a decision to get along with whatever wealth you can accumulate *without worry*.

- Put your foot upon the neck of the fear of criticism by deciding not to worry about what other people think, do, or say.

- Eliminate the fear of old age by deciding to accept it, not as a handicap, but as a great blessing that carries with it wisdom, self-control, and understanding not known to youth.

- Acquit yourself of the fear of ill health by seeking and accepting the counsel of trustworthy medical professionals when needed.

- Master the fear of loss of love by deciding to get along without love, if that is necessary.

Kill the habit of worry, in all its forms, by reaching a general, blanket decision that nothing life has to offer is worth the price of worry. With this decision comes poise, peace of mind, and calmness of thought that will bring happiness.

> # Fears are nothing more than states of mind that can be altered and eliminated.

A person whose mind is filled with fear not only destroys his or her chances of intelligent action, but transmits these destructive vibrations to the minds of all with whom they come into contact.

QUESTIONS TO CONSIDER

1. Before I can put this philosophy into successful use, I must clear my mind of three enemies: indecision, doubt, and fear. Which of the three enemies causes me the most trouble?

_____

_____

_____

_____

_____

_____

2. Indecision is the seedling of fear. It crystallizes into doubt, and the two blend and become fear. There are six basic fears: poverty, criticism, ill health, loss of someone's love, old age, and death. The six basic fears become translated into a state of worry through indecision. Does this describe my mental state?

_____

_____

_____

_____

_____

_____

3. Every human brain is both a broadcasting and receiving station for the vibration of thought. The creative imagination is the "receiving set" of the brain, which receives thoughts released by the brains of others. How susceptible am I to receiving other people's negative thoughts? Positive thoughts?

_____

_____

_____

_____

_____

_____

4. The subconscious mind is the "sending station" of the brain, through which vibrations of thought are broadcast. The broadcasting principle is the factor through which you mix feeling or emotion with your thoughts and pass them on to your subconscious mind. Am I passing along into my subconscious mind mostly good thoughts or detrimental thoughts?

8

AT YOUR COMMAND

A Positive Mental Attitude (PMA) allows you to build on hope and overcome despair and discouragement. By developing and possessing a PMA, you will find your state of mind

is consistently wholesome, healthy, and productive in your reactions to other people and in choosing actions that will lead you to whatever worthy things you want in life. It is no wonder that a PMA is called the "I CAN–I WILL" philosophy.

When you have a positive mental attitude, you are happy with yourself–and with others. You will possess that inner air, that inner light, that inner feeling that allows you to have self-respect and beneficial feelings. You will attract goodwill and circumstances and repel negative ones. The effects of a PMA are automatic, but attaining it is not.

A positive mental attitude requires a continual process of application. It is not something to use at your convenience. It is an essential part of the way you live. A PMA must become a *habit* with you, so ingrained that you demonstrate it always.

By regular application of a PMA, you can practice it without conscious thought, the way you button a button or tie your shoes. It must and can be as natural as breathing. As a road sign in upper New York State once said, "Choose your rut carefully; you'll be in it for the next ten miles." We are all ruled by our habits. Whether your habits and their effects are positive or negative depends on your choices.

You can choose not to allow your mind to be dominated by negative thoughts. You can make a conscious decision to replace negative ideas and impulses with positive ones whenever they occur. Positive habits will automatically influence your mind to be more alert, your imagination to be more active, your enthusiasm to grow, and your willpower to increase.

A positive mental attitude attracts its benefits like a magnet attracts iron filings. PMA will attract people, success, and wealth to you. An optimistic outlook is irresistible. PMA shields and protects you from doubts and hopelessness. When adversity comes into your life—and it visits us all—you will be protected from despair and prevented from being overwhelmed by circumstances. In fact, PMA allows you to see any situation more clearly, so that you can turn adversity into potential success by learning from it and using that knowledge to your benefit.

> **With a positive mental attitude at your command, you think about, act on, or react to each person or circumstance in the right way.**

A positive mental attitude is the correct mental response to any incoming stimulus from your senses. With a PMA at your command, you think about, act upon, or react to each person or circumstance in the right way. Your mind and your life are yours to do with as you deem appropriate.

A positive mental attitude teaches you to think and act constructively. You can use a PMA to bring your wants and desires into reality. When you learn to make the best of what you have, you learn to seize opportunity where others see only a problem. You can put into practice the philosophy of Benjamin Disraeli, the great British Prime Minister: "We are not creatures of circumstance; we are creators of circumstance."

One way to train yourself to act with a PMA is to select a *self-motivator*, a word or phrase that is meaningful to you and reminds you of your commitment to a PMA and the goals you are pursuing. By recalling it to memory often, especially when you find yourself confronting a situation in which a

PMA is especially called for, you strengthen your resolve to act in the most appropriate manner possible.

Repeat your self-motivator aloud many times throughout the day. Say it with feeling and emotion fifty times before you go to bed. Post it where you can see it: on the mirror in the bathroom, on the dashboard of your car, on your desk calendar, on the refrigerator door, in your wallet. The more you repeat it, the more it and the values it expresses become a habit.

> **When you master your emotions, positive emotions will be at your command when you need them.**

SOME WHO NOURISHED A POSITIVE MENTAL ATTITUDE

Many people contributed to the development and refinement of the PMA concept. William James (1842–1910), a Harvard Medical School graduate who stayed at the university to teach anatomy, physiology, psychology, and philosophy, helped to develop a system of thought called pragmatism. According to the ideas of pragmatism, results are what count. Thought is a guide

to action. If a thought does not result in practical actions, it is not useful. James wrote, "Be not afraid of life. Believe that life is worth living, and your belief will create the fact."

The people of James's day respected his theories, and he attracted many followers. He was convinced that life is a battle between pessimism and optimism. James vehemently opposed negative thinking. "It fill[s] people with failure and doubt," he said. The universe, according to James, was full of possibilities. People could vastly improve themselves if they only opened their eyes and looked for the mind power they had within them.

James believed that each of us decides what our future will be and that, "We become what we think about most of the time. The greatest revolution in our generation is the discovery that human beings, by changing the inner attitudes of their minds, can change the outer aspects of their lives."

PMA stands for Positive Mental Attitude, but PMA is more than just an optimistic outlook on life. When you understand it thoroughly and apply it correctly, you will see that it is, in effect, a fourfold process consisting of:

1. An honest, well-balanced way of thinking

2. A successful consciousness

3. An all-embracing philosophy of living

4. The ability to follow through with the correct actions and reactions

A positive mental attitude is "a confident, honest, constructive state of mind which an individual creates and maintains by methods of his own choosing, through the operation of his own willpower, based on the motives of his own adaptation."

So what is PMA? Let's examine the meaning of the three words that form the concept of Positive Mental Attitude:

- **POSITIVE. PMA** is a force or power associated with "plus" characteristics such as honesty, faith, love, integrity, hope, optimism, courage, initiative, generosity, diligence, kindliness, and good common sense.

- **MENTAL. PMA** is a power of your mind, not of your body. Remember, "You are a MIND with a body." Your control is embodied within your mind.

- **ATTITUDE. PMA** depends on the right attitudes, which are feelings or moods. Attitude relates to your basic feelings toward yourself, another person, situation, circumstance, or thing.

The three initial letters combined–PMA–stand for the term Positive Mental Attitude, the adhesive that binds all your plus characteristics, the power source that enables you to be a person who can achieve anything and everything so long as what you desire or do does not violate the laws of God or infringe upon the rights of others. Simply stated, Positive Mental Attitude is the right frame of mind that leads inevitably to the right actions–and reactions.

> **A positive mental attitude leads to the right actions and reactions.**

A PMA is the one stabilizer that you and I need to meet any of life's storms. On a ship, a stabilizer is a kind of shock absorber, a kind of gyroscope that keeps vessels steady in the heavy seas. I remember one trip on a rough sea, but because of the ship's stabilizer, the trip was most pleasant and in no way uncomfortable. On a similar trip, many years ago, the ship had no stabilizer and it was rough, truly rough. But any stabilizer, be it a gyroscope or otherwise, is useless if it isn't used. And so it is with PMA. It must be developed and used.

People who do not develop a positive mental attitude toward life and work become unhappy. Some even develop psychosomatic illnesses, or have nervous breakdowns because they are overwhelmed by any turbulence in their lives. In addition, each of them brings misery to their associates and loved ones.

By developing positive thoughts and eliminating negative thoughts, you use an effective, natural stabilizer that is far superior to any mechanical gyroscope. You have the power to direct your thoughts, control your emotions, and thus ordain your destiny.

I encourage you to put PMA into practice daily, and by doing so, make it part of your life. A Chinese proverb concerning learning says: "I hear and I forget. I see and I remember. I do and I understand." Good advice.

WITHOUT PERSISTENCE, POVERTY

In addition to a positive mental attitude, *persistence* is an essential factor in the process of transmuting *desire* into its monetary equivalent. The basis of persistence is *willpower*.

Willpower and desire, when properly combined, make an irresistible pair. People who accumulate great fortunes are frequently described as cold-blooded—sometimes even ruthless. Often they are misunderstood. What they have is willpower, which they mix with persistence and bolster their desires with to ensure the attainment of their objectives.

> ## Persistence is the sustained effort necessary to induce faith.

Henry Ford generally has been misunderstood to be ruthless and cold-blooded. This misconception grew out of Ford's habit of following through in all of his plans with persistence. The majority of people are ready to throw their aims and purposes overboard and give up at the first sign of opposition or misfortune. A few carry on despite all opposition until they attain their goal. These few are the Fords, Carnegies, Rockefellers, and Edisons, and many modern-day successful men and women.

There may be no heroic connotation to the word "persistence," but the quality is to the character of humans what carbon is to steel. The building of a fortune generally involves the application of the entire thirteen factors of this philosophy. These principles, or steps, must be understood; they must be applied with persistence by all who wish to accumulate money.

If you are following this book with the intention of applying the knowledge it conveys, the first test of your persistence will come when you begin to take action with the six steps described in Chapter 1. Unless you are one of the two out of every hundred who already have a *definite goal* at which you are aiming and a *definite plan* for its attainment, you may read the instructions and then go about your daily routine—never complying with the instructions.

> # Lack of persistence can be conquered; it depends entirely on the intensity of your desire.

Lack of persistence is one of the major causes of failure. Experience with thousands of people has proven that lack of persistence is a weakness common to the majority of people. It is a weakness, though, that can be overcome by effort. The ease with which lack of persistence may be conquered depends entirely on the intensity of your desire.

The starting point of all achievement is desire. Keep this constantly in mind. Weak desires bring weak results, just as a small amount of fire makes a small amount of heat. If you find yourself lacking in persistence, this weakness may be remedied by building a stronger fire under your desires.

Continue to read through to the end of the book; then go back to Chapter 1 and start immediately to carry out the instructions given in connection with the six steps of transmuting your desire into riches. The eagerness with which you follow these instructions will indicate clearly how much, or how little, you really desire to accumulate money. If you find that you are indifferent, you may be sure that you have not yet acquired the "money consciousness" you must possess before you can be sure of amassing a fortune.

Fortunes gravitate to people whose minds have been prepared to "attract" them, just as surely as water gravitates toward the ocean. In this success system may be found all the stimuli necessary to attune any normal mind to the vibrations that will attract the object of your desires.

If you find you are weak in persistence, center your attention on the instructions contained in the next chapter that focuses on the power of the mastermind. Surround yourself with a mastermind group; and through the cooperative efforts of the members of that group, you can develop persistence. You have read additional instructions for the development of persistence in previous chapters on autosuggestion and the subconscious mind. Follow the instructions outlined in this book until your habit nature hands over to your subconscious mind a clear picture of the object of your desire. From that point on, you will not be restricted by a lack of persistence.

Your subconscious mind works continuously–while you are awake and while you are asleep.

Occasional effort to apply the rules will be of no value to you. To get results, you must apply all the rules until their application becomes a fixed habit with you. In no other way can you develop the necessary money consciousness.

> **Without persistence, you will be defeated, even before you start. With persistence, you will win.**

Poverty is attracted to anyone whose mind is favorable to it, as money is attracted to anyone whose mind has been deliberately prepared to attract it–and through the same laws. Poverty consciousness will voluntarily seize the mind that is not occupied with money consciousness. Poverty consciousness develops without conscious application of habits favorable to it. Money consciousness must be created to order, unless one is born with such a consciousness.

Catch the full significance of the statements in the preceding paragraph, and you will understand the importance of persistence in the accumulation of a fortune. Without persistence, you will be defeated, even before you start. With persistence, you will win.

If you have ever experienced a nightmare, you will realize the value of persistence. You are lying in bed, half awake, with a feeling that you are about to be smothered. You are unable to turn over or to move a muscle. You realize that you *must begin to regain control* over your muscles. Through persistent effort of willpower, you finally manage to move the fingers of one hand. By continuing to move your fingers, you extend your control to the muscles of one arm until you can lift it. Then you gain control of the other arm in the same manner. You finally gain control over the muscles of one leg and then extend it to the other leg. Then, with one supreme effort of will, you regain complete control over your muscular system and *snap* out of your nightmare. The trick has been turned step by step.

You may find it necessary to *snap* out of your mental inertia through a similar procedure—moving slowly at first, then increasing your speed until you gain complete control over your will. Be persistent no matter how slowly you may, at first, have to move. With persistence comes success.

If you select your mastermind group with care, you will have in it at least one person who will aid you in the development of persistence. Some who have accumulated great fortunes did so because of necessity. They developed the habit of persistence because they were so closely driven by circumstances that they had to become persistent.

There is no substitute for persistence! It cannot be supplanted by any other quality! Remember this, and it will hearten you, especially in the beginning, when the going may seem difficult and slow.

> # There is no substitute
> # for persistence!

Those who have cultivated the habit of persistence enjoy insurance against failure. No matter how many times they are defeated, they finally arrive at the top of the ladder. Sometimes it appears that there is a hidden Guide whose duty is to test people with all sorts of discouraging experiences. Those who pick themselves up after defeat and keep trying arrive, and the world cries, "Bravo! I knew you could do it!" The hidden Guide lets no one enjoy great achievement without passing the persistence test. Those who can't take it simply do not make the grade.

Those who can "take it" are bountifully rewarded for their persistence. They receive, as their compensation, whatever goal they are pursuing. That is not all! They receive something infinitely more important than material compensation–the knowledge that "Every failure brings with it the seed of an equivalent advantage."

QUESTIONS TO CONSIDER

1. PMA stands for Positive Mental Attitude, consisting of: 1. An honest, well-balanced way of thinking; 2. A successful consciousness; 3. An all-embracing philosophy of living; 4. The ability to follow through with the correct actions and reactions. Considering my normal, day-to-day consciousness and philosophy of living, my level of having a PMA ranks at about _____ percent.

2. The basis of persistence is willpower. The majority of people are ready to throw their aims and purposes overboard and give up at the first sign of opposition or misfortune. The lack of persistence is one of the major causes of failure. I am most persistent when it comes to _____. On the other hand, I have no willpower when it comes to _____.

3. All the steps contained in this success system of speaking it into reality must be applied with persistence. In the areas where I lack persistence, I can remedy this weakness by building a stronger fire under my desire by _____?

4. Without a persistent positive mental attitude, I will be defeated before I begin. With a persistent PMA, I will win. What is the best way for me to cultivate the habit of persistence and enjoy insurance against failure?

_____

_____

_____

_____

_____

_____

_____

_____

_____

_____

_____

_____

_____

9

WORDS FROM THE WISE

This chapter is full of wisdom. Some quotes are from successful people in bygone days, some from today, and all from those wise ones who made a positive difference in people's lives near and wide. You are encouraged to read this chapter with your whole self–mind, body, heart, and soul. And then speak wisdom into your own reality.

"A merry heart doeth good like a medicine."

–Proverbs 17:22

"Cheerfulness keeps up a kind of daylight in the mind, and fills it with a steady and perpetual serenity."

–Joseph Addison

"Assume a virtue, if you have it not."

–William Shakespeare

"Give me a man who sings at his work."

–Thomas Carlyle

"If you want a quality, act as if you already had it. Try the 'as if' technique."

–William James

"Use your weaknesses; aspire to the strength."

–Laurence Olivier

"Study this Book of Instruction continually. Meditate on it day and night so you will be sure to obey everything written in it. Only then will you prosper and succeed in all you do."

–Joshua 1:8

"Peak performers are people who approach any set of circumstances with the attitude that they can get it to turn out the way they want it to. Not once in a while. Regularly. They can count on themselves."

–Charles Garfield

Keep an open mind toward people. Try to like and accept people just as they are instead of demanding or wishing that they be as you want them to be. Look for the good in others and learn to like people.

An essay I wrote for your consideration:

When the dawn of Intelligence shall spread over the eastern horizon of human progress, and Ignorance and Superstition shall have left their last footprints on the sands of time, it will be recorded in the last chapter of the book of man's crimes that his most grievous sin was that of intolerance.

The bitterest intolerance grows out of religious, racial, and economic prejudices and differences of opinion. How long, O God, until we poor mortals will understand the folly of trying to destroy one another because we are of different religious beliefs and racial tendencies?

Our allotted time on this earth is but a fleeting moment. Like a candle, we are lighted, shine for a moment, and flicker out. Why can we not learn to so live during this brief earthly visit that when the great Caravan called Death draws up and announces this visit completed, we will be ready to fold our tents and silently follow out into the great unknown without fear and trembling?

I am hoping that I will find no Jews or Gentiles, Catholics or Protestants, Germans, Englishmen, or Frenchmen when I shall have crossed the bar to the other side. I am hoping that I will find there only human Souls, Brothers and Sisters all, unmarked by race, creed, or color, for I shall want to be done with intolerance so I may rest in peace throughout eternity.

Love and affection generate the mental and physical environment in which a positive mental attitude can flourish. Every day, do a good deed. It's good advice for Boy Scouts, and it's good advice for us.

> "A great many people think they are thinking when they are merely rearranging their prejudices."

> **–William James**

This is a true story:

There was a New England high school student who was an excellent gymnast. He was enroute to a championship meet. As he drove over a certain bridge, he noticed a gap in the railing. He stopped and saw a truck in the river below. The accident had just happened, the truck was still sinking, and the driver was struggling to get out.

The high school youth took off only his shoes, then dived into the swirling waters below. The panicked truck driver couldn't open the door. The high schooler motioned to the driver to roll the window down, for the truck was almost completely submerged. The driver did roll the window down and the youth, from his years of training and exercise, used every muscle and ounce of strength to pull the driver from the truck. He pulled the driver to the surface and swam to the shore, thereby saving the trucker's life.

The gymnast never did show up for the state meet that night, but it didn't matter, for school officials had barred him from the competition anyhow because he had long hair.

The moral: Don't judge a man's character by the length of his hair.

Acts of human kindness condition you and others for the growth of a positive mental attitude. To be happy, make others happy!

"It takes a wise man to recognize a wise man."

–Xenophanes

"Grant that we may not so much seek to be understood as to understand."

–St. Francis of Assisi

"Do all the good you can
By all the means you can
In all the ways you can
In all the places you can
At all the times you can
To all the people you can
As long as you ever can."

–John Wesley

"Nothing is ever lost by courtesy. It is the cheapest of pleasures, costs nothing, and conveys much. It pleases him who gives and receives and thus, like mercy, is twice blessed."

–Erastus Wiman

"There are risks and costs to a program of action, but they are far less than the long-range risks and costs of comfortable inaction."

–John F. Kennedy

"Strong lives are motivated by dynamic purposes."

–Kenneth Hildebrand

"This is the confidence we have in approaching God: that if we ask anything according to his will, he hears us. And if we know that he hears us–whatever we ask–we know that we have what we asked of him."

–1 John 5:14-15

UNAVOIDABLE UGLINESS

Self-suggestion is the process of purposely and deliberately offering stimuli to yourself in the form of seeing, hearing, feeling, tasting, or smelling. Use mental pictures or thoughts as a form of self-suggestion. Under "suggestion," you are warned to see to it that what enters your five senses is wholesome and gratifying. Perhaps the thought occurs to you: "But the world has an unavoidable ugliness in it."

This is just where self-suggestion can come into play, and the underlying philosophy of a positive mental attitude: *look for the good in whatever you see or hear or taste or smell or feel.* The more you purposely repeat a message to yourself, and the more emotion and belief you imbue it with, the more effectively it is implanted in your subconscious mind. By building up successful thought patterns, you can put the same great truth to work for you as so many successful people have done.

> # Look for the good in whatever you see or hear or taste or smell or feel.

Do successful people know some special secret for living? They look for the funny side of things. From this day on, you will too. From this day on, you will laugh off your shortcomings. From this day on, you will refuse to take yourself too seriously. From this day on, you will constantly cultivate your sense of humor by finding something to laugh at each day when you feel a need to relax from tension. From this day on, you will try to attract new friends by a more cheerful attitude. From this day on, you will use humor as an aid to the solution of your problems.

Autosuggestion is the transmission and communication of information stored in the subconscious mind back to your conscious mind. This information returns to you in the form of ideas, dreams, feelings, concepts, principles, solutions, and thoughts. When you deliberately feed your mind with good, wholesome thoughts and information, and keep yourself in the proper frame of mind, you are supplying the subconscious with nourishing material to feed back to you. You condition your mind's output by the input you give it.

Keep a record of each time you notice autosuggestion working for you. It may provide a solution to a problem, or an idea for a new activity. As your record grows longer, you'll have evidence of how your mental attitude is affecting your progress toward success.

> "If you treat a person as he is, he will stay as he is; but if you treat him as if he were what he ought to be, he will become what he ought to be and could be."
>
> **–Johann Goethe**

> "Human felicity is produced not so much by great pieces of good fortune that seldom happen, as by little advantages that occur every day."
>
> **–Benjamin Franklin**

"Put vim, force, vitality into every movement of your body. Let your very atmosphere be that of [one] who is…determined to stand for something, and to be somebody…. Dare to step out of the crowd and blaze your own path."

–Orison Swett Marden

"Aspire to greatness. Each of us is going to travel the road of life's adventure only once, but once is enough if you do it right."

–J. Warren McClure

"What your mind can conceive and believe, you can achieve with a positive mental attitude."

–Napoleon Hill

"He that loveth little, prayeth little. He that loveth much, prayeth much."

–St. Augustine

"Prayer is a sincere, sensible, affectionate pouring out of the soul to God."

–John Bunyan

"I've been driven many times to my knees by the overwhelming conviction that I had nowhere else to go. My own wisdom and all of that about me seemed insufficient for that day."

–Abraham Lincoln

"Let prayer be the key of the morning and the bolt of the evening."

–Matthew Henry

"Prayer is the gate of heaven."

–Thomas Brooks

"It is so natural for a man to pray that no theory can prevent him from doing so."

–James Freeman Clark

"Prayer is the first breath of divine life, it is the pulse of the believing soul."

–T. Scott

"Whatsoever we beg of God, let us also work for it."

–Jeremy Scott

THE EIGHT "PRINCES"—GUIDING PRINCIPLES OF A GREAT LIFE

The princes (principles) serve me through a technique that is simple and adaptable.

Every night, as the last order of the day's activities, the princes and I have a round table session, the major purpose of which is to permit me to express my gratitude for the service they have rendered me during the day.

The conference proceeds precisely as it would if the princes were revealed to me in the flesh, but of course they exist on a higher plane than the physical, and I contact them through the power of thought.

Here you may receive your first test as to your capacity to "condition" your mind for the acceptance of riches. When the shock comes, just remember what happened when Morse, Marconi, Edison, Ford, and the Wright Brothers first announced their perfection of new and better ways of rendering service. It will help you to stand up under the shock.

And now let us go into a session with the princes:

> **Prince of Gratitude,** today has been beautiful. It has provided me with health of body and mind. It has given me food and clothing. It has brought me another day of opportunity to be of service to others. It has given me peace of mind

and freedom from all fear. For these blessings I am grateful to you, my Princes of Guidance. I am grateful to all of you collectively for having unraveled the tangled skein of my past life, thereby freeing my mind, my body and my soul from all causes and effects of both fear and strife.

Prince of Material Prosperity, I am grateful to you for having kept my mind attuned to the consciousness of opulence and plenty, and free from the fear of poverty and want.

Prince of Sound Physical Health, I am grateful to you for having attuned my mind to the consciousness of sound health, thereby providing the means by which every cell of my body and every physical organ is being adequately supplied with an inflow of cosmic energy sufficient unto its needs and providing a direct contact with Infinite Intelligence, which is sufficient for the distribution and application of this energy where it is required.

Prince of Peace of Mind, I am grateful to you for having kept my mind free from all inhibitions and self-imposed limitations, thereby providing my body and my mind with complete rest.

Prince of Hope, I am grateful to you for the fulfillment of today's desires, and for your promise of fulfillment of tomorrow's aims.

Prince of Faith, I am grateful to you for the guidance that you have given me; for your having inspired me to do what has been helpful to me, and for turning me back from doing what had it been done would have proven harmful to me. You have given power to my thoughts, momentum to my deeds, and the wisdom that has enabled me to understand the laws of Nature, and the judgment to enable me to adapt myself to them in a spirit of harmony.

Prince of Love, I am grateful to you for having inspired me to share my riches with all whom I have contacted this day; for having shown me that only that which I give away can I retain as my own. And I am grateful too for the consciousness of love with which you have endowed me, for it has made life sweet and all my relationships with others pleasant.

Prince of Romance, I am grateful to you for having inspired me with the spirit of youth despite the passing of the years.

Prince of Overall Wisdom, my eternal gratitude to you for having transmuted into an enduring asset of priceless value, all of my past failures, defeats, errors of judgment and of deed, all fears, mistakes, disappointments and adversities of every nature; the asset consisting of my willingness and ability to inspire others to take possession of their own minds and to use their mindpower for the attainment of the riches of life, thus providing me with the privilege of sharing all of my blessings with those who are ready to receive them, and thereby enriching and multiplying my own blessings by the scope of their benefit to others.

My gratitude to you also for revealing to me the truth that no human experience need become a liability; that all experiences may be transmuted into useful service; that the power of thought is the only power over which I have complete control; that the power of thought may be translated into happiness at will; that there are no limitations to my power of thought save only those which I set up in my own mind.

My greatest asset consists in my good fortune in having recognized the existence of the Eight Princes, for it is they who conditioned my mind to receive the benefits of riches. It is the habit of daily communication with the princes that insures me the endurance of these riches, let the circumstances of life be whatever they may.

The princes provide me with continuous immunity against all forms of negative mental attitude; they destroy both the seed of negative thought and the germination of that seed in the soil of my mind.

The princes help keep my mind fixed upon my major purpose in life and to give the fullest expression to the attainment of that purpose. They keep me at peace with myself, with the world, and in harmony with my own conscience. They aid me in closing the doors of my mind to all unpleasant thoughts of past failures and defeats and aid me in converting all of my past liabilities into assets of priceless value.

The princes have given me mastery over my most formidable adversary, *myself.* They have shown me what is good for my body and soul, and they have led me inevitably to the Source and supply of all good–Infinite Intelligence. They have taught me the truth that happiness consists not in the possession of things, but in the privilege of self-expression through the use of material things. And they have taught me that it is more blessed to render useful service than to accept the service of others.

The princes have taught me to daily think in terms of what I can *give* and to forget about what I desire to get in return. The princes have taught me to be still and to listen from within! They have given me the *faith* to enable me to override my reason and to accept guidance from within, with full confidence that the small still Voice which speaks from within (1 Kings 19:12) is superior to my own powers of reason. The princes have thus bestowed upon me the master key that opens the gates to the great estate of Happy Valley, and it is my desire to share this estate with all who will condition their minds to accept as much of it as they can use beneficially.

My Creed of Life was inspired by the princes and gifted to me by the King (1 Timothy 6:15). Let me share it with you, so that you may adopt it as your creed, as well.

A HAPPY PERSON'S CREED

I have found happiness by
helping others to find it.

I have sound physical health because I live
temperately in all things, and eat only the foods
which Nature requires for body maintenance.

I am free from fear in all of its forms.

I hate no one, envy no one, but
love all humankind.

I am engaged in a labor of love with which I mix
play generously. Therefore I never grow tired.

I give thanks daily, not for more riches, but
for wisdom with which to recognize, embrace
and properly use the great abundance of
riches I now have at my command.

I speak no name save only to honor it.

I ask no favors of anyone except the privilege of sharing my riches with all who will receive them.

I am on good terms with my conscience. Therefore, it guides me correctly in all that I do.

I have no enemies because I injure no one for any cause, but I benefit all with whom I come into contact by teaching them the way to enduring riches.

I have more material wealth than I need because I am free from greed and covet only the material things I can use while I live.

QUESTIONS TO CONSIDER

1. Of all the quotations cited within this concluding chapter, which two really made me stop and think, made me want to take those thoughts as my own?

_____

_____

_____

_____

_____

_____

2. Self-suggestion involves purposely and deliberately taking the time to see, hear, feel, taste, or smell all the good around me. How often do I insert the time into my day to establish a positive mental attitude?

    _____

    _____

    _____

    _____

    _____

    _____

3. The power of thought is the only power over which I have complete control; that the power of thought may be translated into happiness at will; that there are no limitations to my power of thought save only those which I set up in my own mind. How seriously do I take this power and total control on a day-to-day basis?

    _____

    _____

    _____

    _____

    _____

    _____

4. If I take the Happy Person's Creed as my own, will it change my life: Drastically? Somewhat? Not at all because I already have a life that reflects the tenets of the Creed.

CONCLUSION

Napoleon Hill discovered, through personally analyzing hundreds of successful people, that all of them followed the habit of exchanging ideas. When they had problems to be solved, they sat down together and talked freely until they discovered, from their joint contribution of ideas, a plan that would serve their purpose. They spoke it into reality.

You will get most out of what you learned in this book by putting into practice the positive mental attitude and the mastermind alliance principle. This you can do (as others are doing so successfully) by forming a study club consisting of any desired number of people who are friendly and harmonious. The club should meet regularly, as often as once each week, and should consist of reading one chapter of this book—or any of the Napoleon Hill books available—at each meeting and discussing the contents freely by all members. Each person should take notes, writing ideas that come to mind inspired by the discussion.

Wealth and riches cannot always be measured in money!

By following this plan, you will benefit not only from the sum total of the best knowledge organized from the experiences of hundreds of successful individuals, but more important by far, you will access new sources of knowledge in your own mind as well as acquire knowledge of priceless value from others present.

Remember, riches cannot always be measured in money! Money and material things are essential for the freedom of body and mind, but there are some who will feel that the greatest of all riches can be evaluated only in terms of lasting friendships, harmonious family relationships, sympathy and understanding between business associates, and introspective harmony that brings peace of mind measurable only in spiritual values.

Get ready to experience a changed life filled with harmony and understanding and for the accumulation of wealth in abundance!

Nevertheless, if you understand and apply the steps and adopt this philosophy, you will be better prepared to attract and enjoy higher estates that always have been and always will be denied to all except those who are ready for them.

Be prepared, therefore, when you expose yourself to the influence of this philosophy to experience a changed life that can help you not only to negotiate your way through life with harmony and understanding, but also prepare you for the accumulation of material riches in abundance!

ABOUT NAPOLEON HILL

(1883-1970)

"Remember that your real wealth can be measured not by what you have—but by what you are."

N apoleon Hill was born in Wise County, Virginia. He began his writing career at age 13 as a "mountain reporter" for small town newspapers and went on to become America's most beloved motivational author. His work stands as a monument to individual achievement and is the cornerstone of modern motivation. His most famous work, *Think and Grow Rich,* is one of the best-selling books of all time. Hill established the Foundation as a nonprofit educational institution whose mission is to perpetuate his philosophy of leadership, self-motivation, and individual achievement.

In 1908, during a particularly down time in the U.S. economy and with no money and no work, Napoleon Hill took a job to write success stories about famous men. Although it would not provide much in the way of income, it offered Hill the opportunity to meet and profile the giants of industry and business–the first of whom was the creator of America's steel industry, multimillionaire Andrew Carnegie, who became Hill's mentor.

Carnegie was so impressed by Hill's perceptive mind that following their three-hour interview he invited Hill to spend the weekend at his estate so they could continue the discussion. During the course of the next two days, Carnegie told Hill that he believed any person could achieve greatness if they understood the philosophy of success and the steps required to achieve it. "It's a shame," he said, "that each new generation must find the way to success by trial and error, when the principles are really clear-cut."

Carnegie went on to explain his theory that this knowledge could be gained by interviewing those who had achieved greatness and then compiling the information and research into a comprehensive set of principles. He believed that it would take at least twenty years, and that the result would be "the world's first philosophy of individual achievement." He offered Hill the challenge–for no more compensation than that Carnegie would make the necessary introductions and cover travel expenses.

It took Hill twenty-nine seconds to accept Carnegie's proposal. Carnegie told him afterward that had it taken him more than sixty seconds to make the decision he would have withdrawn the offer, for "a man who cannot reach a decision promptly, once he has all the necessary facts, cannot be depended upon to carry through any decision he may make."

It was through Napoleon Hill's unwavering dedication that his book, *Think and Grow Rich,* was written and more than 80 million copies have been sold.

THANK YOU FOR READING THIS BOOK!

If you found any of the information helpful, please take a few minutes and leave a review on the bookselling platform of your choice.

BONUS GIFT!

Don't forget to sign up to try our newsletter and grab your free personal development ebook here:

soundwisdom.com/classics

Because Your Success Matters